My Footsteps Toward That House

Boksoon Kim

Table Of Content

Preface

I spend a lot of time in my backyard growing plants and flowers. I observed the life cycles of trees, perennials, and annuals. I also observed the life cycles of squirrels, lizards, snails, and other small insects, and recently snakes. All creatures have a life cycle of its own. Each creature lives its own life cycle. During its life and at the end of its life each creature prepares to preserve its kind after their death in forms of seeds, roots, or eggs. When they fail to do it, the species becomes extinct.

Houston has a long hot drought during summer. Snails cover their shells with thin clear layer membranes to keep the remaining moisture for survival. It is their final measure to survive. Usually I find them dried up inside and dead. But before doing that, they already hid their eggs in deep places. As soon as rain comes, baby snails show up. In this way snails have lived on earth for millions of years.

Humans are no exception to this. Just like all other creatures, each human lives one life cycle and has an obligation to pass the human race to the next generation. Humans' one life cycle is; birth, preparation through education and parents' guides, marriage, having a family, sickness and disabilities, and facing eventual death. Each person seeks happiness and prosperity during life time and has an obligation to pass on a better life, better than my own life, to the next generation.

In my mid seventies I am almost concluding my life cycle or my life journey. I want to share my life stories and pass on my stories to the next generation. My stories are not about high accomplishments and successes. My stories are stories of an ordinary person who had a job and worked all life to provide for my family.

I was an ordinary person but my sufferings were extraordinary, too much for me. Why me? I felt that I was the only one suffering in the world. I did not want to live any more. Then later I saw the hidden pains and sufferings of others. Maybe everyone living in this world suffers the similar sufferings I had. I want to comfort and encourage them by sharing my stories. I want to tell them how I overcame so that they may overcome their problems, too.

My stories are far from privileges and luxuries, nothing is fancy. Before I went to the nursery school, I realized that my parents and my family were poor. I had to live like a survivor, learning how to survive from nothing. I can provide the readers and the next generation with my stories on how to be a winner from nothing, how to rise from dirt, and how to fulfill the unfulfilled dreams. I did it and you can do it, too.

I give my thanks to missionary Esther Kim who called me on the phone telling me to write my third book. I give my thanks to Mr. Chris Walter, the project manager, who read my manuscript and encouraged me to write this book. I give my thanks to Mr. Youngchul Hong, the Korean publisher, who helped with the front cover design and the title of this book. I thank pastor John Lee who read my book and encouraged me to publish it. I thank the team in Amazonpublishingnetwork for their work of publishing this book.

09-04-2024

In Houston

Boksoon Kim

Chapter 1:
The Summary of The Three Stalkers

The Stalker #1 In My Hometown

About this stalker I wrote in chapter 2 of my book, 'I asked the author.' In the book I cut the story short. I will tell you the remaining story about this stalker.

After I escaped from my kidnaper to a mountain in the darkness of the night, I went to my friend who lived with her younger brothers. In her room I felt finally safe. She put me at the warmest spot of the room and covered me with several blankets to warm my cold body but I was shaking non stop. My teeth were rattling non stop. I was covered with dirt, the smell of alcohol, bruises and scratches.

The school dormitory had strict rules. At 8pm the dormitory housemaster locked the entrance door to the building. Then all the nursing students lined up in the hallway on both sides of the hall. Then the housemaster began teaching and giving instructions for about ten minutes. After instructions we went to our rooms. At 10pm all the lights should be off and everyone had to be in bed. The housemaster checked each room with her flashlight to make sure everyone was in bed.

While we were studying in classrooms, sometimes our rooms were searched. In the beginning we were instructed to walk quietly with our feet upright. I had a habit of running. So while running I was caught several times by the housemaster.

All students returned to the dormitory before the 8pm curfew. It was an absolute rule. I had not seen a single student who missed the curfew. So I did not know what would happen to a student who had not returned to the dormitory after curfew. Suspension or expulsion from school? I had to return to the dormitory. Being tardy would be a lot better than no show.

My friend knew that I must return to school and she could not do it by herself. Neither my family nor she had a phone. She must have walked to my home at night to let my family know my situation. I don't remember how I met my parents, whether they came to my friend's house or I went to my home.

With my parents I went to school at night. My parents must have knocked on the door of the building. My parents said to the housemaster that I came home from school. I went to a movie theater instead of going back to school, fell on ice and was injured. Graduation was only weeks away. The housemaster and the school accepted my parents' pleas and I was restored to school without any punishment.

My kidnaper almost destroyed my life in a very short time, in a couple of hours, but many helped me to restore my life; my friend, my parents, and the school teachers. And of course, the Lord, even though I did not believe in God at that time. God's protection was already there with me.

I was supposed to work in the hospital as a student nurse. But I had bruises in many places in my body, in my face, legs and knees. So my teachers assigned me to work in a school office to receive applications from new students instead of working in the hospital. It was basically sitting in front of a desk all day long.

Then one day the door of the office slightly opened and I saw a glimpse of the kidnaper through the little opening. I sprang up from the chair and pushed the door so that he might not be able to come in. He was pushing the door from outside to open it and I was pushing hard against it from the inside. It didn't take long. He was stronger than I was. The door opened and he came in.

He dressed up impeccably head to toe. He said; "I saw that you were just leaving" as if nothing serious had happened. He did not say anything to apologize to me, something like, 'I am sorry', or 'Forgive me.' He had no idea how much he hurt my body, mind and soul.

What was his purpose for visiting me in school? Did he think that he could show me a new image of himself with a hairstyle, expensive suit, and shoes? Bull shit! I already saw the dark side of him. There would be no recovery. It only alarmed me that he came to my school without any shame. His visit only warned me that I should go far away from him forever. And I did. I left my hometown, never to see him again.

Almost A Stalker

When I was swimming in the ocean sometimes there were some men, a stranger unknown to me, who tried to catch me in the water. Usually I was swimming far away from the beach. Then I could see one swimming very fast toward me. I immediately knew he was coming to catch me. He was coming fast in freestyle with confidence. But after about 50 meters he became exhausted, using up most of his energy. I was never caught by anyone.

If he couldn't catch me in 50 meters, the situation would turn favorably for me. When any man came closer, I swam away to the deeper sea. That was my strategy to discourage or scare him. He was already exhausted and weak physically. He would be hesitant to go into deeper water. Yet I was strong enough to swim another hour faster than he could. He had to swallow man's pride and returned to the beach defeated.

My favorite swimming style was right side swimming. I put my body parallel with the surface of the water, and squeezed the water with my two legs and with my right arm at the same time. My right arm worked like a paddle rowing a paddle boat. Then my body glided forward on the surface of the water hardly making any splashes.

This swimming style gave me speed as fast as freestyle. I could breathe as much as I wanted because my nose was above the water. I could see everything to evaluate my surroundings. In this style I used less energy than freestyle.

Once I was swimming and I saw a man coming fast toward me. He was lying on his belly on a plastic mattress tube, rowing with his two arms. I couldn't believe that human being. In sport there are rules. Each athlete, all athletes must compete according to the rules. If I swim without any gadget, he should swim without any gadget. But he was coming on a mattress tube while I was swimming without anything. It was like during a marathon everyone is running on foot and one is coming using an electric scooter. He was a man who lacked sportsmanship.

As usual I ran away to deeper water. At some point he threw the mattress tube toward me. I picked it up and threw it back to him and swam away. It seemed like he worried that I might drown. I returned to the beach, put my clothes on and walked a long way home.

The next following story was what I heard from my sister who saw what took place after I arrived home. I did not know that the mattress man followed me all the way from the beach to my home. My home was in a narrow alley. I did not know what the mattress man did, but he was caught by my father. The mattress man escaped my father's grip, ran out of the alley to the main street and my father chased him to the main street. But the mattress man got away.

My sister witnessed all this happening and said to me, "He looked like a scumbag. Why are all men who come after you scumbags? Can you catch someone from high class?" I thought, 'In my poverty level, how can I approach men from the expensive high class?'

That's the end of the story of the mattress man. I did not like his sportsmanship. My sister did not like his look. My father tried to beat him up. He never showed up again near me and my house. He did not become a stalker.

The Stalker #2 In My Hometown

During the senior year of nursing school, sometimes I went swimming at the beach. After final examinations were over, after I saw that I was the top of the class, I celebrated myself by going to swimming. From the school dormitory I walked to the beach.

As usual I was swimming far away from the beach. No one was swimming near me. Then suddenly a man shot out of the water trying to catch me with his hands. He might have been swimming clandestinely under water to approach me. He came very close to me, almost caught me but I ran away from his reach. He shouted loudly, "Ah! Here is a seal!" I saw a glimpse of his face. He was the boss of the gangs whose territory covered all businesses on the beach.

Once he was in the local newspaper being praised as a brave citizen. There was a dangerous situation when a man barricaded himself with a weapon in a second floor room of an inn. The police put the gang boss to subdue the dangerous man. The gang boss went to the roof, opened the window, engaged in a physical fight with the man and subdued the man.

I learned from this news the relationship between the gang boss and the police of the city. They knew each other. They were helping each other. The gang boss gladly accepted a dangerous job for the police and the police did not bother when the gang boss exploited business owners on the beach. I did not know the entire territory of the gang boss. He usually rode a shiny motorcycle and ran fast through the streets of my hometown.

When he could not catch me in the water even with his trick, he did not chase me. I returned to the beach and walked to the school.

After a few weeks, I don't remember how long after, I stopped by my home and was returning to the school. In the street the shiny motorcycle stopped beside me. The gang boss was riding on it. He shoved me to a nearby small alley. He got off the motorcycle and stood right in front of me.

He already assumed that I would know his identity as a gang boss. He roughly cornered me on a narrow street. But when he spoke in front of me, he was a different person. He was calm and serious. He tried to say from his heart. "I am going to be a new person. I will live a new life."

That's what gangs say when they find their love, a resolution of new life. OMG! Am I going to be the girlfriend of a gang boss? I did not look at him but looked at the ground. I did not respond. I just stood there frozen. He said more but I did not remember what he said. Then he quit. He walked to his motorcycle and left. I left for school.

My hometown was small and everyone knew everything. Someone told my father; such, such things happened to your youngest daughter in the street. The street was far away from my home. But people knew whose daughter I was and my father. Ever since whenever I came home my father escorted me to the school gate. He always walked next to me but I did not appreciate my father's protection. I was almost 19-20 years old and I had to walk with my father all the time. When I left my hometown, I was free from the two stalkers, stalker #1, and #2.

A Diamond Man

After I left my hometown I was a midwifery trainee. I was living in Seoul in the nurses' dormitory of the hospital for more than half a year. Somehow I was contacted by a man from my hometown and met him at a bakery store across the dormitory. He was a jewelry store owner in my hometown. I met him once or twice at his jewelry store.

I was responsible for making a contract with a jeweler to make the class golden ring before graduation. I did not know any jeweler. I entered one jewelry store near my house and talked to the owner. I discussed our needs and set the price. Each graduating student had to visit the store and measure the size of her finger. I don't remember meeting him the second time.

That jewelry owner came to Seoul and wanted to meet me. He sat on the other side of the table and I sat facing him. There was no coffee or cakes on the table. Nothing was ordered. There was no warming up. He jumped right into his business.

He said to me, "Please, marry me."

I answered, "No."

"If you marry me, I will give you a diamond ring."

"To me diamonds are just like stones in street, just another stone."

(I felt sorry for him. So I softened the conversation by saying.)

"I am going to go to America as a missionary."

"If you marry me, I will help you and do everything so that you may live as a missionary."

(He did not know what he was talking about.)

"No. I will not marry you."

(He pulled out his last card, more powerful and lethal than diamond.)

"If you don't marry me, I will shoot you with a gun."

(I quickly glanced his hands and suitcase beyond the table. He did not have a gun Then it was my turn to threaten him.)

"If you want to shoot me, do it right now, right here. SHOOT ME RIGHT NOW. RIGHT HERE."

(Everyone in the bakery store heard my yelling. He was not ready for my fearless counterattack.)

He got up and left.

Why was he from one extreme to another extreme?

He had a deep faith in the power of diamonds. Maybe he saw how engagements and marriages ended up successful with diamonds. He came with the power of diamond thinking that I would be knocked out by his diamond. Alas! His diamond had no power on me.

I wish that he might have met a woman who knew the value and the power of diamonds. Then he and the woman would live happily saying, 'Diamond Forever!'

The stalker #3 in N.Y.C.

I finished the Bible study and was returning to my apartment. I was sitting on a wooden bench at a subway station waiting for my train. A young Hispanic boy came and sat next to me. To me he was a teenager. It was okay for him to sit next to me because the bench was for everyone. He asked me, "What is your name?" I did not answer. He asked me again, "How old are you?" I just looked forward and totally ignored him.

But I put my left hand on my lap showing my golden ring in my middle finger. The ring should have given him a message; 'I'm married. Leave me alone.' I bought the golden ring from a street vendor for $1 and wore it all the time even though I was single. That was my idea of keeping myself from the curiosity of undesirable men. It did not work with the boy. He kept on talking to me looking at my face. (All my life I thought the wedding ring goes to the left hand middle finger. Just yesterday 08-01-2024, my friend said that the wedding ring goes next to the little finger.)

Finally the subway train arrived. Many N.Y.C. subway stations were above the ground while some were under the ground. I got up from the bench and got on the train. The boy also got on the same train.

I began to think. First, I had to figure out whether he was stalking me or if he also had to ride the same train. So after a couple of stations I got off the train. He got off also. I got on the next train and he got on. It was sufficient to prove that he was stalking me. I sat on a chair inside of the train and he sat several seats away facing me so that he could watch all my movements.

I was thinking. He should never know the subway station I was using. My apartment was on West 12th street, Manhattan. There was an entrance to the subway station at the end of the street, maybe 11th street. I used this station all the time. I would be in big trouble if he knew about this subway station. I had to cut him off before I arrived there even though he kept his eyes on me constantly.

There was one chance and only chance to cut him off. When a train arrived, the door of the train opened automatically. Passengers got off and got on. Then the door closed automatically. I did not know how long the door remained open and how long after the door closed. My chance was to go out as fast as lightning just one second before closing the door.

It was all about timing. If I exited two seconds before closing, the boy would have a chance to exit after me. But if I exited one second before closing, he could not exit even if he could see me exiting. So I watched carefully several times to feel in my mind how long the door remained open and closed. I rehearsed several times in my mind.

Finally I was ready. The door opened. The passengers got off and got on. I ran out of the door like lightning and the door closed behind me. I quickly turned around. Between the closing doors I saw his blank two eyes and face. He saw me rushing out of the train but he had no chance to come out. The train left and carried the boy with it. Adios! Everything was done in a second. The Lord was on my side. I felt like I was a character in a 007 spy movie. There were tensions, thrills, and a sense of victory of outwitting a villain.

Were these experiences traumatic to my whole life? Maybe. I don't want another stalker. I avoid people. I feel safe when I am alone. That's the reason I stay away from social media.

Chapter 2:
In Front Of That House

In our school music textbooks there were Korean songs chosen and selected as the best songs for students of our time. We were supposed to know and be able to sing those songs. That was a minimal requirement.

One of the songs was a song titled, 'in front of that house.' This song was very strange. From the beginning to the end it was quiet and serene without much crescendo and decrescendo. It was slow and boring. The meaning of the lyrics was very vague. One person was passing a certain house back and forth but eventually stopped in front of that house yet did not want to be noticed that he was there. That's the lyric. I wondered whether the house was a boy friend's house or a girl friend's house.

Then one day I found myself passing back and forth by a house and eventually stopped in front of that house, actually back of that house, and yet did not want to be noticed by anyone. Not a day or two but a few months. Then I fully understood the song and the reason why the song was loved by many. I was doing exactly the same thing as the lyric said. Probably the owner of that house might not know that his house attracted me and was pulling me to his house.

It was in my senior year of high school. In Korea high school senior students focus on studying for college entrance examinations. The study was so hard and competitive for high school senior students that there are expressions like; hell of entrance examinations. Studying everyday from 5am to 11 pm for a year or two is the norm.

Yet I envied those students who were studying like hell because I would not go to college. My parents could not afford my college education. I studied middle school and high school with scholarships but I could not secure college scholarships. It looked like high school education might be my last study. I was roaming and wandering in despair.

The college I really wanted to go to was the art college of Hong University. I wanted to study art. I wanted to be an artist. I did not want to spend my time on academic studies any more. I just wanted to draw and paint day and night all day long. That's what I really wanted to do with my life. But the dream was too far and impossible. Helpless I was but still my mind was drawn to art.

I knew there was an acclaimed, famous artist of Korean art in my hometown. I heard that his house was somewhere on the hill on Yudal mountain. After school, when all my classmates remained at school, were attending extended extra classes for college examinations, I left school and walked toward the hills of the mountain to look for that house. The area was very large in all directions and it was like finding a needle in a haystack. Many alleys on the hills were narrow, curved, separated and joined, up and down.

One day I was passing by houses on the hills and happened to look down at a house over the rock fence. The height of the rock fence was low up to my chest. But the house was sitting much lower than the street level. The house was the average size of a Korean style house. All the windows, not Western style windows but Korean style windows, were open and I could see the oriental artworks hanging on the walls of the rooms. I was not in Oriental art and did not appreciate Oriental art but I was comforted with being close to any form of paintings and art.

My Footsteps Toward That House

I watched the paintings one by one thinking in my heart: 'Someday will I be able to display my art works like that?' I could even smell a faint scent of fragrance in the air coming from that house. I heard later that it was the scent coming from using an Indian ink or Chinese ink stick on an ink stone.

I stood at one spot looking at the paintings for half an hour or an hour until my mind would let me leave the place. Then I left the place and walked toward my home where love and despair were waiting for me. No matter how my parents loved me, their love did not comfort my despaired mind but that house did which had paintings over the rockwall.

I never saw anyone in the house. Actually where I was standing was the back of the house and the main gate was located on the opposite side. I was not sure whether that house belonged to the famous artist or not, but I found solace by standing there and I felt that I was where I wanted to be even over a stonefence.

This visit was abruptly cut off when I had to prepare for the entrance examination for a nursing school. And I never went back to the house again. After school started, I had to study hard to maintain my scholarship for the next three years in the nursing school.

The next three decades I was busy, busy, busy as a mother, as a nurse, as a pastor's wife. But my dream for art did not die in me. When I turned to my fifties, I was thinking: 'Will my life finish like this? Will I ever see my art work?' I was so busy everyday that I would be lucky if I could sleep 4-5 hours per night.

So will I die like this? Am I going to finish my life like this? No! I will not die like this. But I don't have time for art. Then make time. I will never have time till I make time for it. Make time for your art. Yes. I could make time if I wanted to.

I decided to sleep 30 minutes less each day and use the 30 minutes to draw. I was already lacking sleep but I had to do it for my art. I asked my second daughter to buy some art supplies for me. She bought drawing papers, black pencils, a box of black sticks, and spray. That was all I needed.

I finished small group meetings, prayer meetings in the church, dinner, doing dishes, laundry, preparing for children's school, and my work in the hospital the next day. When I finished all the chores, it was usually midnight. All my family was sleeping. It was time for me to go to bed and I was very tired at the end of the day.

But I put the drawing paper in position. I began to draw a woman's face with a black chalk on the drawing paper. It was black lines on a white drawing paper. Light was not bright enough to do any art work but I was happy and grateful for any condition.

I began to realize what I was doing. It was the kind of art of my own which I had been scribbling on a piece of paper since I was a little girl in elementary school. I had no art lessons. I drew small faces with a pencil in any small space of paper.

I always drew a girl's face with a pencil. When I was angry, I drew an angry face, when I was happy, a happy face, when sad, a sad face. In a way my emotions were transferred to the face I drew with a pencil. I didn't know how I did it but my feelings and emotions were revealed on the faces I drew.

I drew small faces, the size of dime or nickel, on any empty space all my life. I got used to drawing small faces. But when I drew on the drawing paper with a black chalk stick, I had to enlarge the size of the faces I was drawing more than a hundred times bigger. It took me a while to draw big faces. When the adjustment was done, I began to draw my own artwork. Each drawing meant a sacrifice of my sleep.

When I drew small faces, I drew only the face. But in a big drawing paper I had to draw the neck and part of the shoulders. Usually artists and art students have a live model, usually a naked woman or a naked man in front of them. They can see and draw. But I had to use my imagination. And it did not work well.

So I decided that I would be my own model. I removed my top shirt and wore only bras. I looked at the mirror from different angles and tried to remember the lines of the curves of my neck and shoulders. I returned to my drawing paper and tried to draw the lines. When I was not sure, I went back to the mirror and looked again.

I put the finished artwork in a frame and took it to work and showed it to doctors and nurses at work. One doctor said, "I went to an art museum and saw a masterpiece painting of a woman. The woman had no feelings but yours is alive." He was right. Every single face of mine conveys a woman's heart. Because I am a woman I know what women feel and what goes through in women's hearts.

One doctor said, "Kim, I never heard that a R.N. starved to death, but I heard of an artist who died of poverty and hunger." Thanks for the realistic comment. I kept my nursing job till retirement and did not go into art further. Indeed, an artist died of poverty and hunger. But after his death his artwork sells millions' dollars and ironically someone else makes a fortune from his artwork. No. I am not going to do that.

One nurse said, "Kim, you drew only white bitches." I thought that I drew Korean women. I did not realize until then most of the faces I drew were close to white women. So I drew one African American woman remembering the face of a coworker at work. I drew the characteristics of her face but beautified it a little. When I took it to work, she immediately recognized that it was her. She asked me to give it to her but I refused. I had to keep it so that I wouldn't be criticized for discrimination.

One said, "You only drew profiles." For the first time I learned the meaning of the word 'profile' in art. It means the side view of the face. The sideline of a woman's face is my signature line. Like a skier runs from the top of a mountain to the bottom in several seconds, I drew the line from top to bottom one or two seconds very fast. I added front faces which I was not good with.

One male nurse selected one drawing and wanted to buy it from me for $50. I did not sell. I drew on it my own experiences of fear and apprehension I had when I was chased by a stalker. I repeated, repeated, again and again until I could reveal on the face the feelings of being chased by fear and anxiety. I can not reproduce it. It was just one and only kind.

But if he had offered several hundred dollars, I might have sold it. But for $50, I would keep it with me. Somehow he liked it among all the other beautiful faces I drew. I thought that either he was drawn to the weakness of a fragile woman in fear or he himself went through a similar experience in his own life. In either way it captured his heart.

I started drawing by sacrificing 30 minutes of sleep each day. In the beginning I kept the thirty minutes. Gradually I stayed awake longer and longer to one hour, two hours and three hours. I was drawing again, and again until I could draw what I wanted. I could not go to sleep until I brought it out on the drawing paper. Bringing out in the paper what I imagined, no one had ever imagined was fascinating.

Is it called an inspiration? When I was in that process, I could not go to sleep. Every creative artist remains as a narcissist until the world joins his narcissism. After the world joins his narcissism, he is called a genius artist.

As I was drawing again, again, I forgot about time. When I drew, I forgot about time, sleeping, drinking, eating, cooking and laundry, my children and family. I drew until I could not stand up but was about to collapse in a disheveled look. Outwardly I did everything I had to do. But inwardly I put all my heart into making a better artwork.

I realized that I would be a very irresponsible person if I were an artist. Had I really wanted to be an artist, I shouldn't have gotten married. At some point I was an indifferent wife, and an indifferent mother. I did not realize the sufferings of my family when I was pursuing my unfulfilled dream. It hurts me as I write this.

I drew about 30 faces. I don't need many. Just one masterpiece will do, and I think that I have at least one masterpiece. But I don't have it with me. I gave my dear friend as a gift. My health was deteriorating and I did not know how long I would live or when I would die suddenly.

I wanted to protect my masterpiece and wanted to put it in the hand of a person who appreciated it. So far she knew the most about the quality and beauty of it more than anyone else and I sent my masterpiece to be safe in her care in case I die suddenly. In a letter to her I wrote; the drawing I gave you is invaluable.

Something came up in my life, I had to stop drawing temporarily but could not go back afterward. But my lifelong thirst for art was quenched. And I found the meaning of art. It gives artistic beauty and satisfaction to me and others, but it does not give life to the dying. People may get artistic satisfaction for a short time from my artwork but my artwork on their wall can not move a finger to help them when they are in trouble.

It is not worth giving my life for art. It is not worth sacrificing family for art. My masterpiece is not worthier than God and my family. I realized that only after I pursued my unfulfilled dream of becoming an artist.

Boksoon Kim

Chapter 3:
A Cup Of Coffee

My parents lived during the last period of the Korean kingdom, the Chosun Dynasty. Things of my parents' generation were different from those of my generation. When the news of the death of the last queen of the kingdom reached the remote village in Pusan, where my father lived, all the village people gathered putting on funeral clothes. They stood together toward the north, toward the palace, bowing down and wailing in sorrow of the loss of the mother of the kingdom.

I was little when I heard that story from my father. I saw how much the village people loved their queen and kingdom, and I felt their expression of the purity of love and devotion. It was a sad story but beautiful. My forefathers were beautiful people.

But the personal relationship between husband and wife was not beautiful. It seemed like that expression of love between husband and wife was not allowed and forbidden. I never heard my father saying to my mother, 'I love you.' I never saw my father and mother holding their hands together. My father and mother always kept a distance of three or four yards between them either outside of the house or inside of the house. In the street my father walked ahead and my mother followed him several steps behind.

Once in a while I saw my mother eating alone in the kitchen while all the family were eating on the table in the room. Later I found myself eating leftovers from family alone in the kitchen and that was okay for me because my mother did the same.

During the kingdom women were not educated. There was no school for girls and women. Education for girls and women started later and my mother did not receive the benefit. My mother lived all her life as an illiterate. And my father looked down on my mother because her understanding of the world was very limited. The conversation between my father and mother was disconnected and short because my mother did not understand the vocabulary my father was using. Men did not want to educate girls and women. How then could they expect a good and wise mother and wife? My mom knew this and she did her best to educate me not to repeat life like hers.

It was very important that women should not speak but remain silent. Women were there to honor men and serve men in silence obediently. Men think women's silent support boosts their confidence, courage and pride. When men failed in what they were doing, they criticized women and did not see their own faults. I grew up under the influence of my parents' life and that was the life I knew. I should not talk back to my parents or teachers or any adults. Only vulgar people with no manners, no respect talk back.

When I came to America things were different. In America only stupid people remain silent. Even empty-headed idiots speak out. I was encouraged to speak. I had to learn to speak out because I grew up thinking that being silent was good. I reminded myself and taught myself that I had freedom to speak out. It is okay to speak out. It is okay to talk back. Talking back is not a vulgar, disrespectful behavior but my right to express myself.

In America expressing my opinion and views are regarded as being intelligent and thoughtful. I liked the American way. I thanked America for teaching me and giving me the freedom and opportunity of expressing my opinions and views. But when I opened my mouth to speak, my words were blunt and abrupt. It took me a long time to learn how to speak and still learning how to speak to others.

Then my husband arrived from Korea. He was also a man under the residue of the tradition of the last kingdom. He walked ahead of me and I followed him from behind in the streets of America. He could not say to me, 'I love you.' Expression of love between husband and wife was forbidden and icky. He was frustrated and angry when I talked about my opinions. All these were okay with me because my father and my mother did that.

However, at work I was in a different world. At work it was a lady first. I was standing in front of the elevator door. The door opened. I would be the last to enter because men would go in first. But men did not go in. A doctor gestured his right hand to me to enter first. So I entered and the rest of the men entered after me. That's at work among Americans; the lady first. A world renowned doctor waited for me to enter the elevator. When I entered first ahead of him and he entered after me. This was No, No in Korea. I would be fired on the spot.

When I came home, I reversed the way from a lady first to husband first. My husband was a very healthy strong man. He walked fast. He did not turn back to see whether I was catching up to his speed or not. With a baby and baby supplies I had to walk fast to follow him. But that was okay with me because that was what my parents did. It took about ten years in America that my husband and I walked side by side. My status improved from behind to equal. He was slowly changing at least in walking.

One day at night I became extremely tired and ready to go to bed. My husband asked me for a cup of tea for him. He had a busy hectic day. Just with me he wanted to have a moment of enjoying a cup of tea served by wife. In a foreign country that was his minimum desire to have as a husband. This was an important part of marriage life at the end of the kingdom in Korea. A husband sits in the honorable seat of the house, and his wife brings a cup of tea in all her calm and submissive manner. He enjoys not only the aroma of the tea but also the calm loving submissive fragrance from her.

I understood what my husband wanted. But honey, I am too tired. I am dying. Don't you see how tired I am! The period of the end of the Korean kingdom women did not work. Women totally depended on men financially. Women were staying at home as homemakers. Serving the husband with tea was an important part of their life.

But sweet heart, look at me. I worked at the hospital. I worked again at home. That's two full time jobs. I also attended church meetings four times a week. If I served my husband with tea, I might die from exhaustion. But I did not know how to explain the situation to my husband.

One day I was reading a local newspaper. There was an article about one day of the life of the president of America. I got an idea from the article. Later when I had a chance, I asked my husband,

"Do you know what the president of America does first thing in the morning?"

He answered.	I answered.
"Watching news on TV."	"No."
"Reading newspapers."	"No."
"Having news briefings."	"No."

"He makes a cup of coffee and takes it to the first lady to her bedside."

The next morning my husband brought a cup of coffee to my bedside. I was numb and speechless. I just looked at him. I even could not say, "Thank you." He was a man from the last dynasty. It might be easier for the whole world to change than for him to change. How could it be possible that he brought a cup of coffee to me? I felt in my skin the invisible influence of the American president and the courage of my husband for change.

The next morning my husband brought a cup of coffee again. I was more relaxed to receive the coffee from him. I was not a coffee drinker. At work I had to choose between coffee or tap water to drink. I chose coffee. But I drank without knowing the flavor or taste. My husband also was not a coffee drinker. He preferred tea. If possible in the morning I prepared his tea which he took to his car and drank while driving. But we kept a drip coffee pot to serve others.

My husband made coffee for me using the drip coffee pot. The next morning he poured the remaining coffee which he made the day before, heated it up, and brought it to me until all the coffee was gone from the coffee pot. I was not at home every morning. When I worked night shift, or day shift I was not at home early in the morning. So my husband brought me a cup of coffee intermittently, maybe 2-3 times a week.

I was amused by what he was doing. I did not want to correct him to make fresh coffee every time. He already did his best more than I expected. I would not try to make him a perfect coffee maker. I appreciated his change from a man from the dynasty period to an American man. One day I saw multiple white dots on the surface of the coffee in the coffee pot. They were fungus molds.

I threw away the coffee and cleaned the coffee pot. I did not tell this to my husband. He continued what he was doing. But since then I drank only several sips.

My husband was a faculty member of a college, teaching math. The college offered free tuition to direct family members of the faculties. So I took one subject each semester. I was sitting in the classroom with all the other students. My husband brought me a fresh cup of coffee from the faculty office to the classroom. When I saw the coffee, my heart was touched.

That was the first cup of coffee he served me during the day besides morning coffee. I smelled the fresh aroma of the coffee and the fragrance of his warm loving heart for me. Months or weeks later he passed away. Since then, I have not had another cup of coffee again like the one he brought to me in the classroom.

Chapter 4:
The Courage To Die Or
The Courage To Live?

After my husband arrived from Korea he took over the ministry I had been building up for two years in the half basement. He gradually changed from Korean centered ministry to American college students' ministry. Life was hard because my income from working at the hospital covered both expenses of my family and a lot of expenses for the church. But there was happiness and joy because the campus ministry was growing.

The joy of a difficult but happy marriage life was brief. First I noticed the changes of the attitudes of the Korean women missionaries toward me. When I was leading the church, they supported me wholeheartedly in what I was doing. They followed the direction I announced.

After my husband took over the leadership, their attitude toward me was a sort of resisting me or ignoring me. My husband had to work with them. My husband had to choose either working with me or working with the women missionaries. When they rejected anything, my husband could not work because they twisted the situation behind him. A leader can not be a leader by himself. When followers support their leader, the leader accomplishes his goal. But when followers don't support their leader, the leader can't do anything. My husband needed their support. So my husband gradually tilted toward them and distanced me.

This continued for several years. My family life and marriage life turned into a nightmare. My husband's love in the beginning of married life became a memory to me. Remembering his love in the beginning of married life, I was convinced that he was a good man but he had been framed.

Remembering the memory of the love of the past was not enough for me to cope with the situation. I was isolated and fighting alone. Criticism about me could be heard and mentioned in conversations of the church members.

When I had back pain, one woman said to me, "God struck your back." These words about me circulated, "She does not pray but thinks." This meant that my word was not spiritual, but a word coming out of my head. So do not listen to her. This subtle word was skillfully designed to disparage me. Not everyone can speak like that. This must have come out of the mouth of an eloquent veteran speaker. I can not remember all the gossip against me. But criticism against me was well established in the church.

I was gradually losing my health. I began to lose my appetite. I did not eat or could not eat. I began to lose weight. My average weight was 123 lbs (=55kg) but my average weight went down to 90's lbs. Bones revealed under thin skins. My husband complained that my skinny look made him feel uncomfortable. He wanted me to gain weight.

I tried to gain weight. In my effort to gain weight I ate one caramel candy whenever I went to work. I bought a caramel candy for 5 cents from a hospital gift shop. Months later I developed seven cavities. My dentist filled seven cavities from both upper and lower jaws. When he gave a dozen shots for local anesthesia, I couldn't hold back tears because of pains. The dentist said to me, "You did the worst thing. (by eating caramel candies)." But I did not gain weight.

Poor appetite was one thing. Another problem I had was insomnia. I had no problem sleeping all my life until then. I worked hard during the day and at night I collapsed to bed and fell asleep in five minutes. But I was not sleepy even though I worked all day. I was very tired but my mind was awake and I was not sleepy. I did not sleep for two or three days but I was not sleepy. I was awake in darkness the whole night.

Then I realized that these were symptoms of depression. I had depression. My mind gave up. I did not want to do anything. Nothing mattered to me. Life was gone from me. I was physically alive but no life in me. I had no hope, no desire, no motivation, no meaning.

I don't know how to describe my mind in depression. It was like I was sitting in a deep hole, I did not want to move, and I did not want to come out of the deep hole. My mind was a vacuum. I was there as a meaningless existence. Those who criticized me looked at me as one punished by God. In such conditions I continued working because I was the breadwinner for my family.

I realized that there was no solution for me. Yet I was looking for an exit from my situation. Life was too miserable. I could not go on in such suffering. What did I do wrong? My sin was that I came to Toledo alone and began to build the church. That was my sin. And they were punishing me for that. I had to be removed so that they could take over the ministry.

I was thinking about suicide. Then I remembered my parents in my hometown. I could not give my parents the worst pain in their lives. So I decided not to commit suicide for the sake of my parents. The problem continued and even got worse. There was no conversation between my husband and me. It was obvious that my husband was regretting his marriage to me but his attitude was that he had no choice but to keep me as his wife. I asked him, "Let's divorce. This is not a married life." He said, "No." He wanted to keep me next to him to cover up his failed marriage life.

I was thinking about suicide again. My parents' suffering did not matter to me any more. I could not continue to live like this. I had to exit from the misery. Then I was thinking about hell. When I commit a suicide, I believed, that I would go to hell. I shouldn't do it. I was afraid of eternal fire. No, I couldn't take it. I decided not to commit a suicide.

Months later I came to convince myself that I did not care about going to hell. I was in hell. I had to come out of the hell I was in. So I finally came to my firm decision to commit a suicide.

I thought that I always pursued truth in my life. I had a freedom to think and a freedom to choose. That's when I was alone and free. Inside of a controlled group I did not have that freedom. Inside of a controlled group one has to choose either to be an obedient follower or a victim. I chose death.

I began to plan my suicide. I needed good preparation so that it might be meaningful and successful. The purpose was to die. But I wanted to hurt my husband more than he hurt me. Killing myself with a gun or knife would not hurt my husband. He would bury me, turn around, and marry another woman. I would be soon forgotten.

I was thinking how I might hurt him all his life through my death. I decided that he should see my dead body, the image of my dead body should be printed in his memory all his life and hunt him all his life. To bring that effect, I decided to hang myself in the kitchen. In the middle of night he would come down to the kitchen for a drink or a snack. Then he would see my dead body dangling. I would wear long loose clothes to look like a ghost. This detailed plan took me about six months and I just had to choose the date.

As I was about to select a date, I was in the kitchen. In the corner of the kitchen, my eldest daughter was standing alone. She was about 5 or 6 years old. Tears were running over her face. She was crying silently. As she was crying, she did not make any sound. I wondered why she was crying like that. Her silent crying bothered me. Children should cry loudly. When I was young crying, I shouted with all my strength so that everybody in the family knew that I was crying. Had she cried loudly, I would not have been so concerned.

She had been caught between my husband and me. My husband ignored me as if I did not exist. I was only thinking about death. She was standing in the corner of the kitchen with tears running over her face, unable to tell why she was crying. Was she hungry? Was she sick? I did not ask her why she was crying. I was thinking. If I am gone, my husband will marry another woman. My daughter will live under a step mother. She will grow up just like that under a step mother, crying silently, standing in a corner of the house, unable to speak about her problems.

It broke my heart. No, I must not let it happen to her. My daughter should not grow like that. My daughter should have smiles on her face. I brought her into this world. I had the responsibility to raise her. My heart was ripped apart by my daughter. Every motive to live died in me but my maternal love was still in me.

I was thinking. I have the courage to die. That required a lot of courage. Do I have the courage to live? That would require a lot of courage for me. Do I have the courage to live for my daughter? Do I have the courage to face and resist the group to bring smiles on her face? Can I go back to my life like hell and decide to live again in hell?

I thought; I had the courage to die. I will have the courage to live for my daughter. I will live. I will live for my daughter. I will fight to live. I will live to protect my daughter. I will live and see smiles on her face. I was determined to live. I came out of a death trap. I came out of the dungeon of depression. I had the purpose to live. I had a desire to live. I think that the Lord brought my daughter there to appeal to maternal love in me and stop my suicide plan.

I had a reason to live. I began to eat. I still had no appetite. But I pushed food into my mouth. I had to be strong to protect my daughter. When my daughter is happy, I will be happy. Gradually I began to restore my physical and mental health. Nothing changed outwardly but my heart changed. My will and my purpose to live were growing in me. I had strength to face harsh treatment and ignorings from my husband and the church members. My face was getting thicker and thicker. Let them keep on talking against me, but I had my own goal to accomplish.

A few years passed. It was Thanksgiving day. There was Thanksgiving dinner at the church. It was a potluck. Every family brought one dish. Everybody sat around a big table and got ready to eat. One woman missionary shouted loudly toward my husband, "You gave us directions yesterday. But you went home and listened to your wife. You changed it and gave us a different direction today after you heard from her."

I could not hold back my tears and I left the place. I did not know what had happened after I left. They might have thanked God and enjoyed the food. I did not know what direction he gave the church the day before and what different direction he gave the next day.

The next day I visited her at her apartment. I politely asked her. "I have not talked to my husband a single word for the last three weeks. Why did you say yesterday that I talked to my husband?" She answered, "Before I left Chicago, (the church director in Chicago) said to me, "Toledo ministry is going down because missionary James Kim is listening to Boksoon Kim." That's why I just assumed."

The church leader's words were regarded as truth, as God's word. When church members acted based on his word, they believed that they were standing on truth. He said that, and so I said that. He did it and so I did it. Their wrong actions were justified by what he said, what he did. They lost not only their own ability of independent thinking but also their consciences in their hearts. But she did not lose her conscience. She said to me honestly.

I suspected this was going on for years. But that day I had solid evidence of a witness. I thanked her for telling me that. I respected her honesty. I liked her because she was worthy.

With the information from her I reevaluated my situation. This was what I learned from the Bible. The first murder in human history was not robbery, love triangle, or revenge. It was a spiritual jealousy of believers of God. Two brothers worshiped God. God accepted one and rejected the other. The one rejected by God killed the one accepted by God. Genesis 4:8. Jesus was killed not by robbery, love triangle, or revenge. It was a spiritual jealousy of believers of God in the temple of God. Mark 15:10

There is jealousy everywhere in human life, in school, at work, in politics, in love affairs, in business, and in every professional field. Spiritual jealousy cut the tape of the first start of murder in human history. When I was in fourth grade in elementary school, for the first time I realized that my classmates were jealous of me.

When a person was jealous of me, I knew it before that person realized it himself/ herself. I smell jealousy when others are jealous of me. I grew up smelling jealousy from others. All I need is two seconds to look at the person's eyes. The jealousy in his/her mind shows in the eyes. Then I keep my distance. Nothing good happens when I am close to them. But in the church I had no place to hide. We had all the church meetings at my house.

Successful person should know that jealousy follows after success. He should be able to handle both success and jealousy. It is like a winning football team has both offense and defense power. Managing success is offense, and managing jealousy is defense. When a successful person does not know how to handle jealousy, his success will not last long. He/she might become a victim of jealousy. When a successful person basks himself in his own success, he is blind to see the approaching jealousy.

When I came to Toledo and started an American college students' ministry, my husband, I were the target of jealousy of believers, yes, of course, the believers of God. My husband was not aware of that and I was aware of it.

When a leader of a group is a jealous person, one should not be a top performer. The top performer will be the target of the leader's jealousy. King Saul's jealousy chased the top general David. The jealous chase followed David and stopped only after Saul died. Then David was freed from the jealousy. When a leader is jealous, one should be a middle level performer to be safe. I wanted my husband to just be a middle level performer but he was a top performer. I worried about him.

The jealous person first removed me by spreading rumors that the Toledo ministry was going down because missionary James Kim was listening to his wife. This was so effective that my husband and women missionaries turned their backs against me.

The next phase would be removing my husband. Finally the jealous person would take over the ministry after removing my husband. How did I know this? That's what I saw happening in another chapter of that church system. In a way my husband was a victim. He lost his wife first by rejecting me and he would lose his position and the ministry eventually. Just he would not know it until the moment he was removed. The day they throw him away would be the day I receive my husband back. I did not know when. But I decided to wait for the day. That day all my family would leave all together.

Years later the day came. My husband was invited to Chicago headquarters and during his stay in Chicago, a missionary in Toledo church announced that he was the new director. My husband was not aware that his position and the ministry were given to another man during his absence. I was not involved in this matter at all so that it might be clear to my husband that my words did not destroy his life. After over a decade I was acquitted from the false accusation. As long as my husband knew it in his heart, it was okay with me.

> *"Even though I walk through the valley of the shadow of death, I will fear no evil, for you are with me; your rod and your staff, they comfort me."*

Psalm 23:4

Looking back on, the misery lasted about ten years. It was the darkest darkness in my life. I was a survivor. I received my husband back. His inner heart was damaged as much as my heart had been once damaged. We left Toledo and moved to Houston.

We lost everything and we had to start from the bottom with wounded hearts. But we had something very good with us. My husband saw my happy face again. I saw his loving eyes toward me again. I saw smiles on the face of my daughter. Whenever I saw her smile I was happy. Her smile was the reason I lived and I enjoyed the fruit of my choice, the courage to live over the courage to die. We started to rebuild our lives again with what we had.

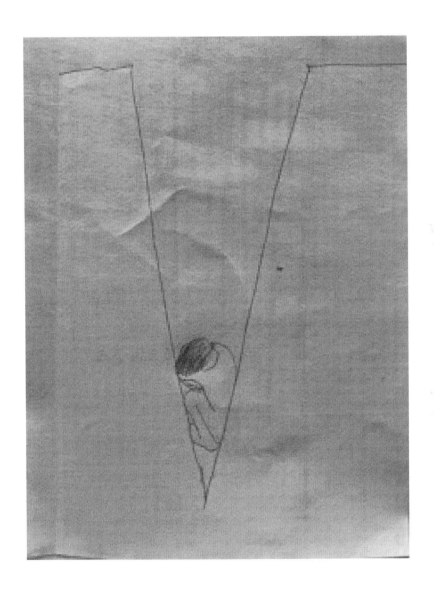

Chapter 5:
Just One Step Forward

It was Saturday and the bank opened in just a half day. I deposited money or a check and left the bank. When I returned to my car in the parking lot, I could not find my car keys. I realized I locked my car, leaving my car keys inside of the car. I walked back to the bank to get some help but the bank was closed and the door of the bank was locked. I returned to my car. Luckily I had my cell phone with me. My husband was out of town. I called my home landline phone. My eldest daughter was at home. She could drive her car and pick me up. But no one answered the phone.

I was thinking whom I could call to get a ride home. Most of them I knew were at work with their weekend jobs. I remembered just one person who might be available. But I could not call her for a ride. Not long ago she called me for a ride for her but I refused. I already gave her rides many times and I wanted her to have her own car. Since then she bought her own car. But because I refused her request for a ride, I could not call her.

Taxi fare might be around $10 but I did not have that money with me and I did not want to spend that money. I decided to walk home. From the bank to home might be 7-8 miles. While walking toward home, I was thinking why the Lord gave me this trouble.

I figured that the Lord knew that I needed money and made me walk to find a bundle of money on the sidewalk. While walking toward home, I carefully watched areas where tall grasses were growing. I found nothing and I realized that was not the intention of the Lord.

I sang for a while and I got tired of singing. I memorized 1Corinthian chapter 15:1-58 in English. I finished it and I got tired of it. I was walking with my legs, but in my head I had too much time and I was bored with too much time.

At that time I had rheumatoid arthritis. My left knee was affected. Sometimes my left knee was swollen and I could not walk. I was under rheumatoid doctor's care and took medicines. I visited a rheumatoid doctor once every two weeks.

During one visit, and my last visit, I asked the doctor. "Doctor, what is the cure for rheumatoid arthritis?" He answered, "If I knew the answer, I would make millions, millions dollars. There is no known cure." Then I asked him, "Then why am I coming here every two weeks?" He answered, "When your knee flares up, then I can help you. I know what to do." That was my last visit. I finished my medicine and did not take any more. I did not return to the doctor.

But I was very careful with rheumatoid arthritis. I stopped eating tomatoes and eggplants which belong to the nightshade family. I bought a package of certo and grape juice from a grocery store for my pain control. I placed an extra pad in my shoes. When I walked, I avoided walking over concrete cement but walked over grasses to lessen pressure between my knee joints. There were times when my knees were aching hours before it started to rain.

So as I was walking from the bank to home, my mind was heavy. I worried whether my knees might hurt. As I approached the half point between the bank and my home, I could not believe that I made that far. I was amazed by my accomplishment. How did I make it? I just moved each step forward. Every step added to 3-4 miles, to an unbelievable long distance. And that was amazing.

Then I thought, "Okay. I can do it. I will just move one step forward at a time." My heart was filled with confidence and hope. It was not hard at all. All I had to do was one step forward from where I had been. Walking the remaining half was light, easy, and joyful. And I arrived home. All together it took me about one and a half hours.

Here, I had a question and I sought an answer for it. I had more energy and better condition when I walked the first half. But the first half of the walking was difficult and hard. For the second half I should have been more tired after walking 3-4 miles. But it was the opposite. Walking the second half was easy, light, and joyful.

Why was it so? By just thinking in my head logically I would be in a better shape in the first half, and I would be more tired in the second half. But in reality it was the opposite. I was more tired in the first half and I was in better condition in the second half. I would have never found this unless I had walked the whole length myself. And that's what the Lord wanted me to walk the whole length. I could learn God's teaching only by going through the whole length.

So what did the Lord want to teach me?

What did I learn?

In the first half I looked at the whole situation as I always had done. How far must I walk? What is my physical condition? How much strength do I have? How much time do I have? I knew this would be a very difficult walk. I might even collapse on the way if I hurt my knee. I was challenging the difficult situation with my determination.

In the second half I learned that each step I moved forward added to the unbelievable 3-4 miles. All I had to do would be moving one step forward. That's all I had to do. The task ahead of me could be done by a simple formula - Just move one step ahead.

It was the difference of thinking. Knowing that I was challenging a very difficult situation was a heavy burden on my mind. I was walking with this heavy burden in the first half. In the second half my thoughts changed. I was thinking in different ways. I was thinking about one step forward and a shorter distance. It was simpler and a lot easier. That knowledge set me free from burden. I realized how easy it is to accomplish my goal!

JUST MOVE ONE STEP FORWARD!!!

That's what the Lord taught me through the trouble that day. It is like moving a rock. I try to move a heavy rock. I assess the weight of the rock and my strength. I conclude that I can not move it and I decide to quit. But if I break the rock into many small pieces and remove them one by one, in the end I can remove it even though it may take a long time. When one way looks impossible, there is another way to do it.

When I arrived home, my daughters were at home. They were watching a movie and did not hear the phone ringing or did not answer the phone when I called them for a ride. I was glad that they did not answer the phone. Had they come and picked me up from the bank, I would have missed the Lord's teaching.

There was a reason why the Lord wanted me to learn about one step forward. At that time we were trying to establish Houston CMI church. There were my family, another family, missionaries Isaac Yun, John Lee. The other family decided to leave the church. So the remaining members were my family, missionaries Isaac, and John.

The departure of one family did not leave a half emptiness, but a whole emptiness and discouragement to the remaining members. With full emptiness and discouragement the remaining members had to struggle to restore our spirits, rebuild the church and I did not want to do it. I decided to close the ministry.

I accomplished everything I wanted to accomplish. I wanted to marry a top elite intellectual man and I did. I wanted to build an American students ministry and I did. I had no more goal that I wanted to give my total devotion. So why should I try to rebuild a church after one family left? My husband could not do anything unless I gave my total commitment to it. And I knew the hardships of building a new church and I decided not to do it any more. It was time for me to enjoy the past accomplishment.

The Lord knew my heart. The Lord was teaching me not to give up. The Lord taught me what I should do.

JUST MOVE ONE STEP FORWARD EACH DAY.

I stood on the ground. I moved my one foot forward where I was standing. I could do it. I moved my other foot forward and I could do it. It was too easy for me to accomplish something in this way. I should not move backward. I should not stay at the same spot. But I should move just a little bit each time each day. 'Yes, Lord, I can do it.' I accepted to serve Houston CMI ministry just in that way, by one step forward each day. I will not go two steps. I will move only one step forward.

Then all the burden, hardships and pressure of building a new church were removed from my heart. I began to think, "From the present situation how can we move one step forward?" There were no challenging decisions, no ten steps, no determinations of faith, no back breaking difficult goals. There was no jump.

We were just a tiny better than yesterday. Tomorrow we will be a tiny better than today.

The change was so little each day that anyone could hardly notice. We were moving forward very, very slowly leaving our future in the hand of the Lord.

My past way of thinking was; I see and evaluate the whole picture.

I set my goals and time.

I push hard myself and people around me to accomplish it.

And it works.

This worked but in the course of doing it, I carried a heavy burden on myself, a high demand and performance from myself and others.

The first victim was my family, my husband and my children. My husband was a super performer. He came from Korea. While serving the church, he finished master 's degree in physics at the University of Toledo and had a job at a college. What other men could have accomplished in ten years, he did it in 2-3 years. But I was not thankful and joyful with him. I did not understand his joy. I wanted him to do more and better.

My first, and second daughters often accomplished the first place in school academically and were national merit scholarship finalists. But I did not know how to be joyful with my daughters' accomplishment because I looked for a higher goal for them.

I don't want to commit sin. But isn't it a sin to hurt my family? My zeal for super accomplishment hurt my husband and my children. My family life should have been a home, a sweet home to them. But what have I done to my family? It hurts my mind.

ONE STEP FORWARD gradually set me free from the obsession of accomplishment. I was able to relax and did just a little bit of what I could do and be thankful for the little move I made and others made. Everything was thankful. Everybody was doing well as long as we moved one step forward each day. After we made one step forward, I could thank the Lord, others and myself. I was thankful for one step forward we made that day. I was thankful for a tiny, tiny thing we made.

I gained this wisdom through walking from the bank to my home. The hundreds thousands and millions of one step added to 7-8 miles.

Chapter 6:
Learning Spanish

In early 1974 I was working in an operating room in Manhattan. A Hispanic male patient was brought into an operating room for a scheduled surgery. He was brought in on a stretcher. His stretcher was placed next to the operating room table. Then the patient would be instructed to move to the operating room table. But the Hispanic patient did not understand English. He did not move and remained on the stretcher.

Some doctors and nurses gestured to him with hands and fingers by pointing and tapping the operating room table. But the patient remained still staring at the ceiling. Some doctors attempted to speak in Spanish but they only proved that their Spanish was not working. The patient did not move.

Then someone went out of the operating room and soon he brought with him one doctor who knew Spanish. He was a Korean doctor who spoke English, Spanish, and Korean fluently. I did not know what other languages he could speak. He was small, short and humble. He arrived and stood by the stretcher and said a short sentence in Spanish.

Then the patient began to move from the stretcher to the operating room table. When the patient started to move, there were jubilant shouts in the operating room. I was very impressed by the short Korean doctor and I decided to learn Spanish. But the next four decades I did not carry out my decision.

My Footsteps Toward That House

Later I moved to Houston where over 50% of the population is Hispanic. Most official documents are written in both English and Spanish. Many are English and Spanish bilingual. Many doctors don't need a translator. They themselves can communicate with their patients in Spanish. I was naturally exposed to a few words of Spanish but not enough to read and speak in Spanish.

Once I was in a patient's room. The Hispanic patient was a minor who did not speak English. A doctor came in. He wanted to talk to the patient's mother. He would come back to see her at three o'clock in the afternoon. Later the mother arrived. I wanted to tell the mother that the doctor wanted to see her at 3pm. I knew tres horas. But I did not know what to say at 3pm. The mom was puzzled about what I meant by tres horas.

Later I shared this experience with my coworkers in the hospital. One Hispanic coworker came to me and said to me friendly; "So, Kim, from now on when you don't know Spanish, don't speak. Don't speak in Spanish. Okay?"

Her comment could be interpreted in different ways depending on the receptors of listeners; as a mocking, or a joking, or an advice. I enjoyed what she said and again I decided to learn Spanish. But I did not carry out my decision.

I was getting old and I had to decide when to retire from my nursing job. I was thinking whether I should retire at age 62 or at age 65. Retirement at age 65 my estimated social security would be $2000 monthly. Early retirement at age 62 my social security would be 25% less. It would be $1500 monthly, $500 less each month.

It was not the amount of money I was concerned about, but the condition of my brain. Will I be able to study Spanish at age 65? Or at age 62? At age 62 I might still be able to study Spanish but I was not sure at age 65. So I decided to retire at age 62 to buy 3 years' time of studying. During these three years I studied both Spanish

44

and theology in the seminary. This was one of the best decisions I have made in my life.

I submitted my resignation from my nursing job at age 62 and the same week I went to Houston Community College to register as a student. In a huge room there were many tables and the college employees were assisting students for class registrations. I took my high school report cards, graduation certificate, nursing school graduation certificate. For some reason I did not have nursing school report cards with me.

The female employee asked me to bring nursing school report cards. I said that I graduated from the nursing school forty years ago and the school did not exist any more. The nursing school turned into a university. I did not have any information about the university. I insisted that high school education was sufficient to register as a student in the community college. She said that since I claimed that I graduated from nursing school, I must prove it by submitting the school reports.

When I argue in English, my voice becomes loud, noisy and angry. So I kept on arguing my point in a loud voice. The female employee totally ignored me and helped the next student. The class of the new semester was to start the following week. I had to start Spanish class the next week. If I could not start, I should go back to work. Even though the female employee ignored me I remained and kept arguing for maybe 20-30 minutes. People in the room knew why the small gray haired Asian woman was upset and yelling.

A young Asian woman, an employee of the college who was in the room, came to me and said to me; if you take the placement tests and pass, you can register and start the class. You don't need your nursing school report card." It was definitely an Asian solidarity. I thanked her and came home.

I called a friend in the church who took the placement test and had necessary information about the test. There would be two tests, English and Math. The English test had a limited time. It was a writing test according to a given subject. Unlimited time would be given for the Math test.

The next morning I went back to Houston Community College and took the test in the testing room. I took the English test first on the computer. Back then I wrote and spoke English better than now. I passed the test. Next I took the Math test. The last time I studied Math was when I was a high school senior, some 45 years ago. I forgot a lot of the basics of Math. I even did not remember which line was X line and which line was Y line. I forgot almost everything except multiplication and division. I was at a loss for a while.

However, I had one opportunity with this Math test. There was unlimited time. So I decided to use it. Okay. I will take all day long and do it. I found a way of solving Math problems which I had never thought of or used before. All problems were multiple choices. There were four answers. One of them was the correct answer. I began to apply each answer to the problem and found out which one was fit describing the question. It took a long time but it worked. It was solving Math problems in the reverse way.

For an easy example; suppose the question was ' What is the answer of 4+7=?'

1. 9

2. 10

3. 11

4. 12

Then I applied 9 to see if 9 satisfied 4+7. Then I applied 10 to see if it was correct. Then I moved to 11. It was to find which answer explains the question. I could not solve all the questions in this way but I was able to find answers significantly. It took me almost four hours to finish the Math test. I passed. 70 was the passing score and I had 73.

I wanted to study Spanish from the very beginning. I took Spanish 101. I went to the first class expecting to study from the very beginning. But I faced a nightmare that I had never expected. There were about 25-30 students in the class. In Houston, Spanish is taught in regular classes in middle and high schools. All students in the classroom had a certain level of knowledge of Spanish. I was the only one and the last one who did not take any Spanish classes before. So the professor did not explain in detail which most students had already learned.

I had to catch up with the class by self study. There were two classes a week and I spent the whole week in self study. I felt like my head was all tangled and going to explode. Probably many may quit at this point.

But I persisted, always sitting in the front row and giving my full attention to the teaching of the professor. One student asked me; Kim, how old are you? " I answered her: "Multiply your age by three." My head did not explode but the stress level was gradually going down. I studied five semesters over two and a half years. That was all the Spanish courses in the Houston Community College System. I had all A's.

One foreign language brings the abundance, riches, and history of the people who speak the language. So I love the taste of Mexican foods, the harmony of music, and their sun tanned faces with warm hearts. But they speak too fast for me.

The biggest gain was to learn about queen Isabella. My homework was to write about a Hispanic hero. I typed Hispanic heroes. There appeared a long list of names. I read the unfamiliar names one by one. I came to a female name. She was the only female among all the men. So I wanted to know about her. It really opened a new world that I did not know before. She accomplished a lot but I want to mention about two things; terminating the Moslem rule out of Iberia peninsula and the support of the expedition of Columbus. I think that all Europe owed their prosperity to Queen Isabella.

Studying a language is like playing the piano. Everyone who wants to play piano, starts from the very basics of moving ten fingers. After practicing everyday, fingers gain flexibility and strength. Practice continues weeks after weeks, months after months, years after years. Then one becomes an accomplished pianist. There is no jump. To become a pianist one has to practice and repeat numerous times everyday for years. When one stops practicing piano, he loses everything that he built up for years and so is studying a language.

Frequency is the key. Practicing Spanish one hour everyday for ten days is better than studying ten hours in one day and none for nine days. Studying twelve minutes everyday for ten days is better than studying two hours in one day and studying none for nine days. It is because the brain requires repetition to remember.

Not to lose what I studied for two and a half years, I read CNN Espanol everyday on Youtube. I read the Bible in Spanish and pray in Spanish. God does not mind when I make an error in my Spanish when I pray. I can read and understand. I can say what I want to say. But I can not answer because I don't understand what they are saying. Hearing is difficult. Twice I edited myself the Spanish translated version of my book, I Asked The Author.

Chapter 7:
My Painful Heart

When our body is sick, there is pain in the body. The sick person goes to a doctor to be healed. After sickness is healed, the pain goes away. Every sick person wants to be free from illness and pain.

But when one's heart is painful, what can be done to be healed and be free from the aching pains of heart? People take pain medicines to relieve physical pains. Are there any pain pills to relieve the pain in one's heart? Do antidepressants heal the pain in the heart? Do flowers and condolence cards relieve the pains in one's heart? Good for them if flowers and cards healed the pain in their hearts. In my case pain remained in my heart.

My baby son was born with a congenital heart disease. He had several heart surgeries and lived a short life of six months. Nothing comforted my heart. I will be comforted when I go to heaven and hold him in my arms.

After many years I lost my baby daughter in a car accident. She just started to walk a few steps. When I came back from work, she crawled to me, and wanted me to hug her. Normally I hugged her. But that day I didn't. I had time to do just one thing before I went to the Bible study, to hug her or to do dishes in the sink.

My father-in-law was visiting us and stayed with us. He expected that everything would evolve around him fit for the head of Kim's family. And it was not. He was unhappy with me and complained about many things to my husband. His complaints made the already bad relationship worse between my husband and me. To lessen his complaints I chose to do dishes instead of hugging my baby. She crawled to me and began to cry behind my legs. I thought I would have many, many years to hug her later, but she was gone.

I stretched my arms to hold her but my arms were empty. I wanted to feel the heavy weight of her in my arms but my arms were empty and light. Nothing comforted my heart. I will be comforted when I go to heaven and hold her in my arms. That's the only way to heal my painful heart.

My sister told me that my mom lost three children. Two sons were sick but couldn't have medical treatment during World War 11. One baby girl died of starvation. I wondered how my mom lived her life with deep pains in her heart.

Since then I could not hold any baby or young child in my arms. I just could not hold a baby in my arms anymore. I could not even go closer to the babies. I stayed away from babies. I could not explain why. Just something in my mind rejected babies. Two of my babies were taken away from my arms. My arms were empty. It was impossible for me to hold a baby anymore.

One missionary family had a baby girl, their first baby. I stayed away from the baby. Her parents interpreted my action as my rejection of their child and I did not love their baby daughter. I did not as they thought. I could not. I lost the ability to hold babies in my arms.

According to Korean culture, the pastor's wife should express love and affection to their baby. But they noticed that I was staying away from their baby. I did not explain to them the reason why I did not touch their baby. Even if I explained to them, could they understand? Could they see and feel the pain in my heart if I explained to them? Eventually they left the church. I believed that one of the reasons was that they believed I did not love their baby.

After many years my husband passed away. I knew that his death was coming. I had a dream. In my dream he and I were sitting about 3-4 feet apart. We were sitting toward opposite directions, his eyes were on the other side and my eyes were opposite sides, each facing just backs. Even though we faced our backs, we were talking amicably back and forth. Then suddenly there was silence from him. I turned around to see why he stopped talking to me, I saw his dropped head backward over his shoulders. His face was dead.

I wished that this dream wouldn't come true. I kept no secret to my husband but I could not tell this dream to my husband. It was a freak accident from what he was doing in my dream. I looked into my husband's daily life and tried to find out any possible danger that he could be exposed to in a freak accident.

I identified that. It was his fishing boat. When he took a fishing boat to sea, there were many unexpected dangers. Whenever he went out with fishing boat, I panicked. My husband knew that. So as soon as he arrived from the sea to the land, he called me first to let me know his safe arrival.

After about one and a half years since I had the dream, my husband went out with his fishing boat. He had three guests in his boat. He returned from fishing and arrived at the parking area. He called me when he arrived. But he never returned home. On the way home, while driving the van with the boat tied, he had a heart attack.

Once in a while I told him, "How many years can we live together? Ten years? Twenty years? Eventually we will separate when one dies. So let's live happily every moment with our best, with the most of it." As usual he had no response to my words but I knew he heard it and thought about it. Some time later he said to me, "You suffered a lot. From now on you will sit on a silk cushion and enjoy your life."

We fought with each other for many years. Then we stopped fighting and began to serve and help each other. Then I realized that we don't live forever together. We should make the most of our lives together for the remaining years we have. When I realized it, and my husband realized it, he was gone.

I was helpless. I felt that a fence protecting me crumbled down and I was exposed to the world. The thought that I was alone in this world made me feel helpless. I was left alone. Only more pains were added to my heart. My life was hectic as a pastor after him. But when I was alone, the pains in my heart started to ache.

Fear within me increased without my husband, especially at night. I lock the front door and back door. I made sure that sixteen windows around the house were all locked. I locked the bedroom door. And I pushed a chair against the bedroom door from inside. Then I was able to sleep with fear, loneliness and pain.

Then my first grandson was born, my daughter's first son. After her maternity leave finished, she went back to her work. I began to babysit my baby grandson around four hours a day. I was kind of concerned about my inability to hold a baby. But I was able to hold my grandson in my arms. He was so small. I was able to hold his small body in my two hands. He slept most of the time. He drank milk and slept. He pooped and drank milk and slept. He farted and slept. He yawned and slept.

As I was looking at his sleeping face, his sleeping face was purity itself. The purity and peace from him spread around him. The purity and peace of him began to seep into my heart. I liked his smell. I sniffed the baby smell from him. His smell was a fragrance to my heart.

As he grew 2-3 months old, his eyes followed my face. One day I was holding him in my arms. He reached out his tiny finger and touched my neck. That was a gesture that he recognized me. He was expressing his desire and intention to communicate with me even though he could not speak a word yet. What was in his heart? What was he trying to express? The touch of his finger was an angel's touch that transcended any other communications I had in the past.

Day by day I had some communication with my grandson, communication between his grandma whose heart was filled with pain and grandson who just came from God into this world. He brought purity and peace from heaven and was sharing them with me. His tiny finger touched my face more often. Every time he touched my face, I felt an unspoken message from him, better than thousands of words of grown-ups. As snow melted in the sunlight, the pain in my heart began to heal.

I raised my daughters and my son. I did not have such times with my children. I was always rushing to take them to babysitters or daycare in a hurry and rushed to work. I missed all their baby times. This was the first time with my grandson finding out that babies brought untouched, untainted heavenly purity into this world. And that purity began to heal my heart.

When he was about six months old, he began to talk. His first word was 'car.' Whenever he saw a passing car, he said, "car." At around 10:30 am a dozen yellow school buses passed the nearby street. A school must be near.

Watching the passing of the school buses one after another was an important daily event. I took him outside to watch the passing of the school buses. Each time a yellow school bus passed, I said, "school bus." But when a car or cars passed, I said. "Car." He could not pick up the compound word, school bus. But he picked the single word, car. Even inside of a room when he did not see a passing car, he said," car." He knew the meaning of car. He could not pronounce 'school bus,' but he knew what it was.

He began to call me, 'halmoney,' which means grandma in Korean. He went through a few steps to pronounce it. He said, 'halmi,' then 'halmimi,' then finally 'halmoney.'

I finished babysitting him when he was about 5 or 6 years old. He began to go to school. By the time the pain in my heart was healed.

Flowers do not speak a word. But by watching flowers people receive beauty, comfort, and pleasure. My infant baby grandson did not speak a word yet. But when I watched him, and watched his face, he brought me life, love, and healing. He does not know that he gave his halmoney healing for her painful heart. He did what no one could do for me. Someday he will read this, and realize what a great gift he brought from heaven to his halmoney.

Chapter 8:
Finally Retirement

I retired from nursing years ago but maintained the pastor's position a few years more. And finally I submitted my resignation from the pastor's position. The church leadership offered me a monthly retirement payment but I refused to accept it.

The reasons of my refusal was;

1. I knew how hard each of my church family was working. I did not want to live with their sweats and hard work. I would not be able to swallow my food with a comfortable heart.

2. I wanted to keep my freedom of decision. I tried to keep this freedom all my life like a treasure. I want to say 'yes' when I have to say 'yes.' I want to say 'no' when I have to say 'no'. This freedom does not come naturally because I want to have it. I have to be careful of what I say and do. My own actions and words support my view even later on. This freedom comes after I fight for it with courage and pay a heavy price for it.

But when I receive money, the money that I receive influences my judgment and I lose power to make the right decision. I would be dragged by the money I received. I did not want to fall into this disgrace at the end of my life.

3. I receive monthly social security payments. If I do not receive social security payment, I would accept retirement payment from

the church. I earned it and I deserved to receive it. But I receive the social security payment monthly, I will live with it and I will adjust my life to live within the social security payment. I got used to living frugally.

The retirement life was amazing and I loved it. There were no deadlines, no planning, no requirements, no expectations, no worries, no weight on my shoulders, and no goal. The word which I lived with all my life 'I must' was gone. Instead of 'I must' I lived a new life with 'whatever I want'. I got up whenever I wanted, went to bed whenever I wanted, no limit in time, space and activities.

What is a proper word to describe this kind of state? It is not freedom, rather a state of vacuum, a world of no rules, unlimited indulgence. It was like walking and wandering in weightless gravity on the moon. It was like an ox jumping around when a yoke is removed. I have never lived in such a state since my birth. It was not bad, and it was a new world to me. Growing succulents got me some routines.

The unlimited indulgence came to an end. I began to have health problems. I began to see straight lines crooked. Anything straight was no longer straight but distorted here and there.. The straight lines of roof top, the straight window frames, the electric lines.... ect were all crooked. I wondered why. Finally after a couple of months I visited an eye doctor.

After many eye tests the diagnosis was a macula hole. Macula hole is one of the common diseases among old people. Doctor showed me a picture of my eye. There was an open hole in the retina of my left eye and a surgery was scheduled. Anyone with this symptom should see an eye doctor right away sooner the better. The hole becomes only larger and eventually the person loses vision of that eye or has poor vision.

I was a little late to see the eye doctor. In my case after 2-3 months lingering, the success rate of surgery drops to 60%. Because of Covid 19, five days before the surgery I had to have a Covid test. If positive, the scheduled surgery would be canceled. So I refused to meet anyone. I did not go near anyone. My surgery shouldn't be delayed or canceled by trying to be polite and kind to others who wanted to visit me during Covid 19.

Someone called me on the phone to see me. She was outside of my house. She would put her mask on and talk to me 2 feet away from me. I said, No. I should not have any chance of cancellation of my eye surgery.

The surgery itself was simple. I slept during the surgery and woke up when it was completed. But the recovery was hard. I had to keep my head down 24/7, day and night, for one week including sleeping time. My son-in-law, James, rented from a medical supply store a metal chair where I could sit and lean my head face down for a few hours at a time. I faithfully used different eye drops with different frequencies. I had to keep an eye shield all the time.

After one week I visited the eye surgeon. It was the day I waited to remove the eye shield and see again with two eyes. He examined my left eye in all directions with bright light. "Cataract started as a complication. I could not see the surgery site in the back." So my left eye remained blind after the surgery. I needed an additional surgery to remove the cataract. But I had to wait 4-5 months until my left eye healed from the surgical wound. Until then, my left eye remained without vision and the result of eye surgery for the macula hole was uncertain.

Before eye problems I had problems in my right hand and fingers. Something was not right with my right hand and fingers. I diagnosed it myself as a carpal tunnel by using my hand a lot in gardening. I bought a carpal tunnel brace and used it. But it did not help. One day I was sitting on the floor of my living room doing nothing. My fingers in my right hand twitched in all directions involuntarily. After a few days both my fingers of right hand and toes of my right foot twitched in all directions.

I went to see a doctor. My neck bones were collapsing. There are spaces between each neck bone and nerve bundles pass through the spaces. Since the space was collapsing and narrowed, the nerve bundle was squeezed causing involuntary twitching of my fingers and toes.

The neurosurgeon said that a neck surgery would be the only treatment.

But I wanted to try physical therapy to correct the problem. The physical therapy went smoothly twice a week for about 2-3 months until I almost threw up. That day the exercise I was doing involved my neck. I became nauseated and sick to my stomach. I felt like I was passing out. That was the end of the physical therapy.

I was scared of complications from neck surgery. I read about stories of unfortunate people who had to live with complications after neck surgeries. But I had no choice but to return to the neurosurgeon. Involuntary twitchings would only increase in frequency and severity. Surgery was 50/50, either success or failure. I put my hope in 50% success and decided to have neck surgery.

Between eye surgeries while waiting for 4-5 months for the next eye surgery I had the neck surgery. In the good old days patients with spinal surgery stayed in hospital 1-2 days for recovery and observation. But in more developed medical systems of today patients with neck surgery went home the same day and recovery was done at home. After the neck surgery in the hospital I was discharged from the recovery room to home at around 1- 2pm. My friend Judy was at my home to care for me.

At around 7-8pm my whole body began to shake uncontrollably. All my teeth were rattling and arms, hands, legs, and body were shaking and jerking. It was not shaking coming from being cold, but shaking coming from sick body conditions. I was sitting in my bed. I could not think anything because my brain also went down together. But I thought. 'Should I call 911?'

Then I realized that I was beginning to go into hypoglycemic shock. Because of the pain and swelling in my throat I hardly drank anything after surgery. I did not drink the night before. The remaining sugar in my body was all used up by the stress of the surgery. I drank a little bit in the recovery room. But since then I did not drink anything all day. I figured that my blood sugar level was hitting dangerously low levels.

I asked Judy to give me a cup of orange juice with two spoonfuls of sugar in it. While shaking I forced myself to sip drop by drop the concentrated sugar juice. This was a race between hypoglycemic shock and sugar juice depending on which one went faster. Shaking lasted another one or two hours and finally subsided.

When the shaking was over, my whole body was aching. I wondered how lay people who are not trained medically handle postoperative recovery at home. They may call 911. By the time a patient arrives in hospital, the patient will be in ICU with hypoglycemic shock. I also could have been lying like a vegetable in the ICU but the Lord answered all the prayers of church families for my surgery.

After that my recovery went smoothly. I wore a cervical collar around my neck for a long time.

I went to the first check up after the operation. The neurosurgeon was very pleased with my healing and recovery. Once I did not follow and trust his words. I went on my own way only to delay the treatment. I returned to him almost after 6 months in worse condition. He was not bitter or hurt. He welcomed me when I returned. He did the operation for me and was happy with my recovery. I thanked him in his office and I thank him again in this writing.

3-4 months after the neck surgery I went back to have cataract surgery of my left eye. I read about cataract surgery as much as I could. I learned one thing about eye surgery. Surgery itself is quite simple and short. But recovery is long and patient's understanding and self care are more important.

Patients must study and understand. That's the key to successful eye surgery.

One single importance is not to get infection by avoiding water in the operated eye during 1 or 2 weeks. But I did not wet my operated eye for 4 weeks. I wiped with a damp towel around my eye, and I never, never allowed a drop of water into my operated eye.

I went to post operation check up to the surgeon who did cataract surgery on me. She said that the cataract surgery was successful, and the macula surgery was also successful. How beautiful, sweet, and wonderful to hear the news! I spent almost a year for three surgeries. She said that the eye surgeon who did macula surgery on me asked her to let him know the result of macula surgery. She said that she would call him soon and let him know that his macular hole surgery on me was successful. I felt I was so loved by my doctors.

Between two eye surgeries I lived with one eye vision, my right eye. With one eye I lost the ability to feel distances. When I drove my car I could not tell the distance between my car and another car. I felt like I might hit the other car next to my car. Because of this fear I stopped driving. When I poured water from a pitcher to a cup, I thought that I was pouring water into the cup. But actually the water did not go into the cup but spilled over the table.

I could not see things in detail but vaguely. When I saw my plants and succulents, I could not tell whether there was fungus infestation or insect infestation. Worms might be eating leaves as usual but I could not see any. I began to see everything as one whole rounded object; house, car, tree, man, woman, boy, girl, baby, dog, cat....... I could not see each distinctive character. I tried to read the Bible using a magnifying glass. But I felt stress in my right eye. I thought that I should not stress my only remaining vision but keep it safe. So I stopped reading the Bible.

I was gradually moving into a strange, unfamiliar world. I was alive but everything was vague. I was doing minimal activities for survival such as eating, moving, sleeping, and even talking. But I was losing mental acuity. Everything was cloudy and muddy. The world was spinning fast. But I did not care. I no longer was interested in processing new things. I was alive and moving. That was all and I got used to it.

When I recovered visions in both eyes after two eye surgeries, I felt that I returned to the real world. I resumed driving my car again. I went grocery shopping again and I did not have to depend on others for my grocery shopping. I read the Bible again without causing stress to my eyes. It was like green fresh shoots coming out in early spring. I was thankful that I could see with two eyes. I was thankful that I could read the Bible again.

After three surgeries in a year I began to think that I might not have enough time left in this world. I began to prepare for my departure from this world. I downsized my belongings to minimal necessity. I prepared my will. I wanted cremation instead of burial in the ground. I wanted a quiet exit from this world without bothering anyone.

As I was thinking about death in detail every cell in my body, mind, and soul was also dying under the power of death. The power of death overshadowed me. I was only thinking about death. Some retirees enjoy their retirement. Good for them! My retirement was a series of illnesses and preparation for death.

Chapter 9:
How About Writing A Book?

Missionary Daniel Kim went to Korea to visit his family. On his way back he brought me a gift of a pillow which his parents-in-law sent for me. Maybe they heard that I had neck surgery. It was a special pillow. Missionary Daniel Kim came to drop the pillow to my house at 7pm on August 13th, 2023, Sunday. I had not seen him for a long time. So we talked for about two hours. During conversation he said to me, "How about writing a book?" I did not respond to his suggestion because I did not think about writing a book. Anyway we finished our conversation and he left at 9pm.

His casual comment; 'How about writing a book?' sank deeply into my heart as an imperative command from the Lord. As soon as he left the door of my house I grabbed papers and ball point pens and began to write. It was going to be my autobiography. I spreaded out on my bed; papers, a clip board, dictionaries, and pens. I knelt down and leaned on the side of the bed.

I went back to my childhood in my hometown. I began to recall events I went through. But I had a clear direction. I wanted to introduce God through my autobiography. I was not going to narrate all the events I went through. I selected events that showed God's presence in my life.

I forgot a lot about things that had happened in my life 60-70 years ago. So while I was writing I constantly prayed to the Lord, "Lord, what happened at that time?" Then I could remember things I forgot. At some point thoughts came to my mind very quickly like flash and left my mind very quickly. I knew something came in but I was not quick enough to grasp it and it was gone.

So when any thought came to my mind, I quickly wrote just the first word in the paper so that I might be able to recall later. I felt that the concentration and spirit I had had when I was young, returned to me. I wrote in Korean because things happened in Korea in Korean.

Remembering forgotten events was one thing but writing in words was another thing. So I prayed, "Lord, how can I write this in words?" My writing style was always; simple, clear, and powerful. What I wanted to say I rearranged so that the story would be simple, clear, and powerful. Anything that is simple and clear is powerful.

For one simple thing, people scatter all over and make it complicated using difficult vocabularies. After reading repeatedly I understand what the beautiful complicated sentences meant. My job is to make it simple. In order to write in a simple, clear, and powerful way sometimes I use a metaphor. Then I prayed to the Lord, "Lord, how can I compare this with?" A perfect metaphor came to my mind. Then I, myself, was surprised by it. 'Wow, it is that simple.'

I don't remember how long I was sitting in the same position. Maybe a few hours at a time. I continued praying and writing. I did not have Korean alphabets to type on my computer so I wrote on papers with ball point pens. My right arm started to ache and my folded legs numb due to poor circulation. Because of prolonged sitting in folded legs I developed circulation problems in my right leg.

I continued writing day and night praying and writing. At some point I heard a Korean word, 'Dae Bak', which means a big hit. So from that moment on I knew that my book would be a big hit.

I started writing at 9pm Sunday and finished the book at 7pm Friday the same week. It took 5 days minus 2 hours. My book has a total of 18 chapters. I wrote 15 chapters during 5 days and later I added 3 chapters.

The reason I hurried to finish my book in five days was that I wanted to show it to missionary Daniel Kim when he came back Friday. He said that he would come back Friday at 7 pm. When he came back Friday evening, I gave him my handwritten manuscripts of my book.

I waited for his response to my book. If his response is negative, I would stop there and not publish it. If his response is positive, I would continue and go ahead toward publication. His response would determine the future of my book.

He returned my manuscripts after about ten days. I saw that his heart was touched by my book. I was convinced. I started my journey of writing and publishing an autobiography. I began to translate the writing into English. In the beginning of translation I was not confident in my English. But Google docs corrected small errors for me and it was a big help for my translation.

I knew nothing about writing a book. I knew nothing about publishing a book. I stepped into the unknown future of publishing my autobiography.

Chapter 10:
You Will Write Your Second Book.

My first book, 'I asked the author' was on the way for publication both in Korea and in America. My church friend, Hae Hun Matos, stopped by my house briefly. Right before leaving my house she said to me clearly, "You will write your second book." When I heard that, I said to myself, "I don't think so." Writing a book is not easy. I suffered a lot. I did not want to go through it again.

As time passed, I realized that I had more untold stories to tell. I wrote the first book to introduce who God is. It was for young Christians and beginners. I did not want to put heavy contents in the book, which may confuse or burden some readers.

I had stories that I really wanted to share with full time Gospel workers who have given their lives to serve God. There are principles in serving the Lord. The principles are very simple and clear. But many miss the simple principles. And life work and life devotion do not bear much fruit.

I was in the front line of the mission field for over fifty years. Over fifty years I could observe the beginnings and the endings of each missionary's life and ministry. There are very simple principles which some missionaries missed in their ministry. I wanted to share those, my knowledge, my observation, for the next generation Gospel workers.

I wanted to write my second book as a guide book for those who give their lives to serve the Lord. I want them to bear abundant fruit at the end of their life and ministry. I do not want them to feel empty with no fruit at the end of mission life.

Readers may read my first book quickly. But readers of my second book need to read each chapter slowly, thinking about the meaning of each chapter deeply because in each chapter I put the principle using my life experience. Each chapter requires meditation. Otherwise, they may miss my point. Readers with speed reading will learn nothing.

For example, in my first book I wrote about banana bread. It was a story about how I made banana bread instead of serving rice cakes. The meaning behind this story is how missionaries need to overcome cultural differences. Korean missionaries go to a foreign country. They grew up in Korea in Korean culture. A lot of them maintain Korean culture and die in Korean culture.

In my chapter of banana bread, I maintained eating and serving rice cake. But when I saw a boy throwing away rice cake, I realized that I was serving as I wanted, not the boy wanted. So I switched from serving rice cake to serving banana cake. In this chapter I was trying to talk about a missionary's adaptation of the culture of the mission field.

I began to gather subjects that I wanted to explain using real experiences of my own life.

I began to remember each event. Of course I had to pray for God's help to remember and record accurately. My mind traveled back to the past event and my mind was participating in the event as in the past. It was a kind of reenacting.

God's power and love filled my heart like a tsunami. The awesome surprising feelings came to my heart vividly with the same intensity as I had had in the past. The words God had spoken to me in the past returned to my heart. The joy and excitement I had had in the past did not diminish at all. It all came back when I was writing.

Before writing the two books I was wandering in the shadow of death because of health problems one after another. The whole year I was thinking about death. Every cell in my body, mind, and soul was dying under the power of death.

After writing two books I came out of the shadow of death. Every cell in my body, mind, and soul became alive, not just being alive, but full of life, power, and love of God. I have been rejuvenated in body and soul. From thinking about death to thinking about God I crossed over from death to life after or through writing two books. People around me noticed my changes.

I did not notice the changes within me after I wrote the first book. But after writing the second book, my inside was in heaven. Maybe that's why the Lord wanted me to write the second book. The darkness was totally expelled from my inside and heavenly joy filled my heart.

Mr. Hong, the Korean publisher said, "Usually a writer writes and publishes one book a year. But you wrote and published two books within months." My friend Hae Hun who triggered the writing of the second book said, "You wrote your second book as fast as lightning."

Chapter 11:
I Think That You Will Write Your
Third Book.

My cell phone rang. It was missionary Esther Kim calling from St. Louis, Missouri. She asked me, "What do you want me to do with the two chapters?" I asked her, "What two chapters?" She said, "You just sent me today." I answered, "No. I did not send you anything today. Maybe months ago if I had sent it." She meant two chapters of my first book. So the situation was I did not send anything to her that day but she received something in her mail (I am not sure whether it was her computer mail or a package mail.) and she did not know what to do with it.

Regardless, we began to talk casually over the phone. At the end of the conversation she said, "I think you will write your third book." She explained why but it was not clear to me over the phone. After I hung up the phone, I was lost. I did not know what to think about it. After writing two books I really felt that I had nothing left to write more. For a while I did not think about it.

After several weeks I began to think about it. I had a couple of chapters I wrote before but I did not include either in my first book or the second book. The reason was that I wanted to introduce God in my books but these two chapters were about me. In a way these two chapters were disqualified because they were about me and not about God. They were a part of my life stories which some readers may be interested in reading. The title of the two chapters were, 'The summary of the three stalkers' and 'Learning Spanish.'

I wanted to show these two chapters to someone who can give me feedback. My project manager, Mr. Chris Walter, was willing to read them. So I emailed him those two chapters. His response started with "Wow." He recommended that I include them in my third book. I was encouraged and I wrote another chapter. The title was 'In front of that house.' I emailed it to Mr. Walter. He recommended that I include that in my third book. So I began to write more and more.

I called Mr. Hong, the Korean publisher and let him know that I am writing my third book. He encouraged me to write. Anything I write I want him to read first because he has a keen literary sense and he can see my book from readers' perspective. But I could not show him because I have been writing in English and I have not yet translated into Korean, but told him that it is about my own life.

My personality is fearlessly challenging and persistent. Whatever I do, I do my best, and risk my life for it. Readers may feel it through reading my first, and second books. Now, I am in my mid seventies. I want to write more subdued gentle stories like on the road of life's journey, sharing my stories with those who walk their own life journey.

I prayed to the Lord that each chapter may spread like ripple waves in a lake of each reader's heart.

Chapter 12:
Finding Publishers

I knew nothing about the publication of a book when I started writing a book. After finishing the writing, I had to find a Korean publisher for my Korean manuscript. How can I find a Korean publisher while I live in Houston in isolation? Pastor Mark Hong introduced me to one Korean publisher living in Korea. We communicated through Kakao talk.

He gave me advice on what to do. First, type the handwritten manuscript in Korean. Second, find a person who can edit it. Third, find a person who can put the edited and typed manuscript in format. Fourth, bring it to him for printing. He does only printing. According to him, I needed to go through four steps; typing, editing, formatting, and printing.

I did not try to find a person who can type my handwritten manuscript in Korean for free. I did not want to ask any one in the church to type it for me. Everyone has a job and works hard. It would be a burdensome request. I wanted to hire someone with pay. But where in Houston can I find a person who can type my manuscript in Korean? There might be a lot of Koreans in Houston who can type but I just did not know how to find them.

I contacted my nephew living in Chicago. He has a wide connection with Korean friends. He asked me to send him the picture of the first several pages which I did. He contacted some people for my book publishing but nothing was done. I thought that publishing a book from an unknown author was not an appealing business.

Then I wanted to help someone through my book. I began to pray to the Lord that I want a Korean publisher who prays to the Lord and who needs financial help. There is a well established Christian publisher in Korea. They have manpower, strong finance, and established distribution routes. They don't need my help. I wanted to help a small publisher with my book. This was my opportunity to help someone.

I did not know how I could find such a publisher. I live in Houston, and the unknown publisher is in Korea. How can I find that publisher? God can bring two strangers to meet together for His good purpose. That's what the Bible says.

a.　　　When baby Moses was crying in a basket in the Nile river, the princess of Egypt came out to the river to bathe. She heard the baby crying. The totally different strangers met together. Was it a coincidence or God's sovereignty?

b.　　　When Abraham's servant was praying for a bride for Isaac, Rebekah came to the well. The totally different strangers met together. Was it a coincidence or God's sovereignty?

c.　　　Saul's father lost a sheep. He sent out Saul to look for the lost sheep. Saul went out. Prophet Samuel was coming to anoint Saul as king. The two strangers met in the field and prophet Samuel anointed Saul. Was it coincidence or God's sovereignty?

d.　　　Philip met the Ethiopian. Acts 8:26-40

e.　　　Saul met Ananias. Acts 9:1-19

f.　　　Cornelius met Peter. Acts 10:1-48

I believe that God is living and God can bring two strangers to meet together. That's what the Bible says not once or twice but throughout the whole Bible. I believed that God could make one Korean publisher and I would meet. So I trusted in God's Sovereignty in this matter and kept on praying.

One month, two months passed. This was the most difficult time throughout the whole publishing process. Just waiting without a publisher. I regretted that I specifically prayed for a publisher who prays to God and who needs help financially. I should have just chosen whichever publisher and move forward.

So I checked the big Christian publisher in Korea. I entered the web site and read information and guidelines. All manuscripts have to be typed before submission. Two weeks after receiving the manuscript the publisher would decide whether to accept to publish or not and the writer would be notified of their decision. I just mailed my handwritten scripts to the publisher in Korea. I did what I could do.

After a couple of days I was on the phone with missionary Esther Kim in St. Louis. During conversation she asked me, "Do you have a publisher for your book?" I answered, "No." She said, "I think my brother in law in Seoul has a publishing business." She called her brother in law in Seoul right away and introduced him to me through Kakao talk. He said to me, "First, send me your manuscript and I will read it. And I will decide." So I mailed my handwritten manuscript to his address in Korea. His company name was Hongyoungsa.

So I sent my manuscripts to two publishers in Korea; one big Christian publisher, and the Hongyoungsa. I prayed to the Lord that one may accept and the other may reject. If both of them want to accept, I would be in trouble because I would not know which one to choose. If both reject, I would be in more trouble. So the best way for me was one to accept my book and the other to reject it.

It took about one week to receive my package in Korea. Mr. Hong, Hongyoungsa called me. He liked my book and he wanted to publish my book. So I asked him the cost of publishing and to send me a contract. I knew in my heart that God led me to him. God works in a mysterious way.

He emailed me a contract using a commonly used standard contract form between publisher and writer. I read it and requested to change the contract period from five years to two years. The publisher was still unknown to me and I did not know with whom I was making a contract. So I wanted to have a shorter period of contract. He accepted my request and sent me a revised contract.

Then the Lord warned me about the revised contract. So I began to read each sentence of the contract carefully. And I found a sentence which might cause a problem later unless clarified. The sentence was this; the writer gives the copyright of the book 'I asked the author.' to the publisher. I was thinking of translating and publishing this book into many different languages. If I give the copyright of the whole book to the publisher, I would need publisher's permission whenever I published it in a different language. That's a literal interpretation of the sentence.

So I asked Mr. Hong to limit the copyright to only the Korean version. Mr. Hong emailed me another revised contract with copyright limited to the Korean version. So I signed the contract. I still missed one point but at that time I had no ability to discern it because of my lack of experience in publishing. It was out of my scope of understanding at that time.

Finally I was able to solve all four steps of preparations for publishing; typing, editing, formatting, and printing by the service of Hongyoungsa.

After all these were done, the big Christian publisher emailed me that they decided not to publish my book and wished me good luck. As I prayed, one publisher accepted my book and the other declined.

After that I was looking for an American publisher to publish the English version which I finished translating. Since my computer skill was limited, I was looking for a walk-in publisher whom I could see face to face, eye to eye, and communicate in words instead of emails.

I typed publishers in the Houston area. The list of the top fifty publishers showed up on the computer. From the addresses I chose streets I knew around in my area. Houston is a large city and I hate to be lost. I also chose publishers with ground parking. I hate to be lost in parking buildings. I selected four publishers with a history of twenty years, thirty years in business. I would choose one from the four.

I called one publisher on the phone. The phone was not in service. They were out of business.

I called the next publisher on the phone. The phone was not in service. I called the third publisher. The phone was not in service. I called the fourth one. They publish only medical related articles. The conclusion I got was the small independent publishers were out of business.

I had no choice but to go to online publishers. I really hate anything online. One of the reasons was my poor computer skills. Another reason was that many scammers work online. Scammers as publishers would ask money and disappear after collecting money. I did not want to be a victim like some writers who posted their bitter experiences.

Unwilling yet cautiously I was looking for a publisher online. I was looking for Kindle publisher which everyone was talking about. I thought Kindle was a part of Amazon. So I typed Amazon to look for Kindle. There were so many Amazons, Amazon something, Amazon something, Amazon something, Amazon something I did not know which one was Amazon I was looking for.

Out of many Amazon somethings I clicked Amazonpublishingnetwork thinking this must be the publishing department of Amazon company. There was a chat room. I typed my situation. Answer came right away with a positive comment. I said that I was not good at computers. The answer said," Don't worry. Someone will call you soon and guide you step by step."

I waited for the phone call. Not long after, someone called my cell phone. His name was Chris, one of the project managers of Amazonpublishingnetwork. I thought that finally the Lord led me to the publishing department of Amazon. Later I found out that Amazonpublishingnetwork is a totally independent publisher and is not associated with Amazon.

Mr. Chris Walter provided me ample time to guide me. I had 18 chapters typed in English stored in Google doc. Mr. Chris Walter guided me to send one by one to his email. I followed his guide and was able to send all eighteen chapters to his email. From the beginning to the end it took about 20 minutes.

It was an amazing experience. Up to then my way was I would have printed out over one hundred fifty pages of papers, put them in a mailing envelope and gone to the UPS store to mail the package. Fear and hatred in technology in me was changing to acceptance and thrill. By clicking at home I could save money, time, and driving.

So the publication of my first book 'I asked the author' started via an online publisher. Again in a mysterious way the Lord guided me to meet the publisher for the English version.

Chapter 13:
One Arrow For Shoot-Off

Some grow up with plenty of opportunities. Rich parents provide their sons and daughters with the best opportunities for their future. Others grow up with no opportunity. Poor parents can barely provide food to eat for their sons and daughters. I grew up with no opportunity. However I was keenly aware of the value of opportunity that I did not have and what I should do when an opportunity came to me. When I wanted anything, I had to make an opportunity myself and I did my best to do it.

Young girls of my age asked their parents to buy them dolls. Then parents ran to the store and bought dolls for their daughters who began to play with the dolls happily. I did not have that. When I wanted a doll, I made it myself. With old socks, a pair of scissors, needle, thread, and cotton, I made a doll. I attached arms and legs. I drew a face and black hairs. I made doll clothes. Other girls knew how to play with it but I knew how to make it.

I did not have an opportunity but I worked hard. When others worked once, I worked ten times more. When others worked ten times, I worked one hundred times. I found that this extraordinary hard work pays up and is quite effective.

When an opportunity rarely comes unexpectedly, I know that it is my chance and it is my one arrow shoot-off. In archery competitions, when the competing two archers have the same score, each archer can shoot one arrow. The last one arrow determines the winner and the loser.

It is just shooting one time. But behind the one arrow the archers have practiced shooting hundreds thousands times. Shooting five hundred times a day is the norm for Olympic preparation. That means one has to shoot one shot every minute for eight hours a day for months or years. After that kind of practice in real competition an archer stands to shoot one arrow shoot-off.

Last mid April pastor Mark Hong said to me that there would be a celebration of the publication of my books during CMI International Bible Conference in July. My five senses immediately recognized that this would be my one arrow shoot-off opportunity. Missionaries will come from all over the world and I will shoot my one arrow.

Forty minutes were allocated for the celebration of the publication of my books. I made a program for forty minutes. Then I heard one hour was given. I changed to a one hour program. Then I had to change back to a forty minute program.

Besides the overall program I prepared my own testimony which I was going to read during the program. My testimony was my one arrow for shoot-off. I had fifteen minutes to present it. As one who had no opportunity in life I put all my efforts when an opportunity was given. I was not going to present my testimony like a practice shooting. I would present it as one arrow of shoot-off.

After I wrote my testimony I repeatedly read it over and over again. It was because English was not my native language and I wanted to pronounce it accurately. When I repeated about one hundred times, I naturally memorized all, every sentence and words.

Next the second hundred times I practiced speed, volume, high and low tones. Most preachers in English speak at a slow speed. But I had only fifteen minutes. When I tried to say everything I wanted, I had to speak fast, and that was not good either. I had to remove a whole section to speak at a comfortable speed for the audience.

Next the third hundred times I read thinking about the audiences; teenagers, college students from America, Korea, and other nations, older missionaries. I selected, changed words according to their terms and interests.

Next fourth and fifth hundred times I aimed at their hearts and souls. During this period I watched America's Got Talent. The audience did not have a reaction to some singers. The same audience became wild, standing, shouting, and clapping to a certain singer.

What made the difference? I thought about it and came to a conclusion. First, the sensational singer had a good voice. Second, the singer was able to deliver the emotion and message of the song. The emotion and message of the song were successfully delivered to the audience and touched the hearts of the audience. Humans have hearts. Humans respond when their hearts are touched.

Finding the reason for the wild response from the talent competition was like finding a hidden treasure to me. This was an important discovery to me. My testimony had my emotions I went through and messages I wanted to speak. When I speak, my emotions and message have to be with my words. So I practiced speaking with my emotions and message when I spoke.

How can I do that? I can do it just like the sensational singer. The singer understood and digested the emotion and message of the song. The singer had the same emotion and message in his own heart while singing. Simply, he sang from his heart delivering emotions and messages, singing sad songs sadly, happy songs happily, and love songs expressing love.

So when I read my testimony, I should not just read. I should infuse my emotions and messages from my heart when I read. So my fourth, and fifth hundred times I practiced that.

During these practices I had swellings inside of my lips and face. Swellings in my face went down during the day but swellings inside of my mouth were persistent. I thought I developed an allergy to a certain food. I tried to identify the food and started to stop eating certain foods one by one; oatmeal, chives, perilla leaves. But the swelling persisted. So I began to eat again all the foods I stopped. The swelling did not come from food allergies.

I made a doctor's appointment. I did not want to present my testimony with swollen lips and face in the conference. But the day I had a doctor's appointment, hurricane Beryl passed Houston and the whole city had a blackout. All medical clinics were closed and my doctor's appointment was canceled.

I went to the conference hoping that my swellings might not get worse. After I returned from the conference, I was able to see a doctor. He did not find any problem. He advised me to change my dentist and change my dentures. He did not know that I use my partial dentures only for eating. I did not agree that using dentures for a short time causes my swelling.

I still have swellings. It just did not get better or worse. I still think that it happened because I used my mouth too many times, over five hundred times, to read and practice.

I did not count how many times I was reading over and over. When my condition was good, I repeated over ten to fifteen times a day fifteen minutes each time. When I was tired, I read only four or five times a day. I did it everyday over two and a half months and I continued after I arrived at the conference place. That was my part, and I did all I could do. But that was not enough.

I invited the Lord. I wanted the presence of God. I said to the Lord. "Lord, I attended two college graduation ceremonies last May. I saw fathers, mothers, and families who came to celebrate the graduation. Some fathers skipped their work to come to the ceremony. I am your daughter and you are my Father. Shouldn't my Father come to the daughter's celebration of the publication of her books?" I emphasized to the Lord that I am His daughter and He is my Father. I invited the Lord repeatedly to the last moment.

My program was scheduled at 3pm Friday. On Friday during lunch time I sat next to Mrs. Sookchul Hur who came from Korea to attend the conference. I told her how I prepared my testimony by reading over five hundred times.

She answered me, "When a speaker speaks in a tense mood, the audience will feel the same tension in their hearts. When a speaker speaks in a comfortable mood, the audience will also feel comfortable in their hearts. So relax and deliver your testimony in a comfortable heart." I accepted her words. I delivered my testimony with a relaxed, comfortable heart. I said to myself, 'It is okay to make some mistakes.'

So that day I shot my one arrow shoot-off, leaving the result in the hand of the Lord. It was a rare opportunity given to me and I did my best.

Chapter 14:
God Opened The Door Of
Prison Ministry

Editing and publication of my first book were in the process both in Korea and in America. I had frequent conversations with publishers via phone call and emails. After I talked to them my frustration grew. They did not pray for what they were doing. I remembered what I read from the web site of the big Christian publisher in Korea. I read that they pray before they start to work and pray after they finish their work. That is exactly what I do whatever I do. That's how I receive God's help, guidance, and blessings on what I do.

But the Korean publisher and the American publisher did not pray to God as they were working on my book. How could they expect God's help for my book? They were depending on their business skills and experiences in the world of publication. They just knew what to do next according to their already established system. They did not seek blessings from God. They depended on marketing strategies for the success of a book.

They did not know that all things depend on God's blessings. When God blesses, books will be successful. When God does not bless, books will live shortly and become obsolete. Even though I prayed every day for my book and both publishers, I was frustrated by the fact that they did not pray to the Lord.

Once I was talking to Mr. Hong, Hongyoungsa publisher in Korea. I talked to him about my future prospects for my book in Korea: About how many Christians there are in Korea. If 10 % of them buy my book, how many books may be bought? I mentioned this to him so that he may be prepared for the future, for the bright future.

He tried to talk to me about reality. People do not buy books nowadays. They spend money for concerts, recreations but they do not want to spend $15 to buy a book. He tried to convince me to regard my publication as personal accomplishment and memoir, not more than that. To him I was dreaming out of reality. Looking at reality without God is all negative. Nothing can be done.

Kindly, cautiously, and patiently he explained to me who left Korea fifty years ago and did not know the present reality in Korea. I understood what he said. What he said was true. But I don't follow the world. The world should follow me. I am showing the world how to come to God, and they should follow the way I show them. It is a matter of eternal life or eternal death.

Once after I hung up the phone after the conversation with him, I was a little upset. I prayed to the Lord. "Lord, show him who You are. He does not know how great You are. My God whom I believe is almighty. Nothing is impossible with my God. Let him know who You are." I was determined that I would not go anywhere but hang around him until he sees the glory of God. I will prove to him who my God is.

I felt sorry that I put my book in the hands of people who did not pray. It was my autobiography. But it was also about the words of God because I wrote how I followed the words of God. When they handle the words of God, they should pray before and after their work. But they did not. I was apologetic to the Lord. I felt that I did something wrong to the Lord. I had no choice but to choose them. What else could I have done?

I prayed a lot before choosing a publisher and I was convinced that I followed God's lead to choose both the Korean publisher and the American publisher. Despite my prayers, how did I end up putting my book in the hands of people who do not pray? I could not understand it. My mind was heavy and I was sorry for having chosen them. But I prayed everyday for my publishers, Mr. Hong in Korea and Mr. Chris Walter, the project manager in America. I prayed for them to come to the Lord and I blessed that their publishing businesses may be blessed through my book.

After I prayed for them for two or three months I heard that Mr. Hong came to the Lord. He used to go to church but stopped. He started to attend church worship services again on Sundays in Korea. I didn't know that because he did not mention it. I cried and cried loudly because God loved him and gave him faith in his heart.

God revealed His love for Mr. Hong. The amazing God's love reached Mr. Hong during editing, not even before the book was published. The joy was so great in my heart that I was happy and satisfied all day long for several days. God's salvation has come to my Korean publisher. I joined the joys of the angels in heaven.

Mr. Chris Walter was talking as an aggressive publisher telling me about how to market my book and tips on making money. I did not feel the spirit of the Lord from his words. I was convinced that he might come to the Lord if he would read my book. I decided to challenge him to read my books. At that time my first book was published and the second book was in the process of publication. He had my second book file in his email.

I asked him, "Chris, did you read my book?" He answered, "No." I was determined to ask him ten times until he read it. If he would not read it after my ten requests, then I would ask him another ten times, another ten times....., until he reads my books.

After several days I asked him again, "Chris, have you read my books?" He answered, "Yes." I heard his changed voice, different from before. He did not talk as a businessman. He talked as one whose heart had been touched by God. He read my second book, 'The Half Basement.' And the Lord touched his heart.

I cried and cried loudly because God showed His love for Mr. Chris Walter, brought him to the Lord out of this world. God's salvation has come to my project manager. The angels in heaven rejoiced with me because one more soul came to the Lord.

Then the puzzle was solved: Why didn't God put my books in the hands of the big Christian publisher who pray before and after their work but put my books in the hands of the publishers who don't pray. God did not make a mistake. It was God's plan to send my books to them. The Lord put my books in the darkness and my books were shining the light of God in the darkness. My two publishers came to the light of God. I was amazed to realize God's way of working.

We do not need light in bright places. We turn on light in the darkness. Light does not need light, but darkness needs light. Had my books gone to the big Christian publisher, my two publishers would have remained in the darkness. But thank God that He put my books in the hands of present publishers and brought my publishers to Himself.

God is amazing. How could I fathom the way of the Lord? God has been doing right from the beginning until then but I kept on apologizing to God in my frustration because I did not understand what the Lord was doing.

"For my thoughts are not your thoughts, neither are your ways my ways, As the heavens are higher than the earth, so are my ways higher than your ways and my thoughts than your thoughts."

Isaiah 55:8,9

Everything was clear. The Lord put my books in the darkness and let them shine the light of God in the darkness. Since that was what God was doing, I would do the same thing. I will send my books to dark places. Originally my distribution plan was targeting Christians and churches. But I changed the original plan and direction. Christians and churches are already in the light of God. My books should be sent to the dark, dark places, to the darkest dark places on earth to shine the light of God in the darkness.

Where is the darkest dark place on earth? My answer was a prison. I think we all face our own darkest darkness at some point in life. When we face darkness, we still have freedom and provision of necessities. But people in prison face the darkest darkness without freedom and necessary provisions. How dark can it be inside of prisons? There is the darkest darkness of humans. I hope all prisoners may know that the Lord is with them because the Lord turned the direction of my book from the light places to dark places.

From that time on I began to pray to send my books to prisons. I began to pray to send 1000 of my books to every prison in Korea, 2000 of my books to every prison in America. I began to read articles about prison life. It was more scary than I could handle. I would not go close to prisons. But the Lord was heading to prisoners and so I was also turning to prisoners. I can not imagine and comprehend the depth of love of God for those incarcerated. God's love is like the air in the sky, like the water in the ocean in every life.

I calculated the cost of sending my books to prisons, 1000 books in Korea, 2000 books in America. I calculated roughly that the expense would be $50,000. I did not have that money. Should I ask for donations from others? I really did not want to do it. I'd rather not do it at all.

So should I quit even before I start anything because I don't have the money and I don't want to solicit donations?

Then the words of God came to my mind. John 6:1-13 about Jesus fed the five thousands.

Jesus asked the disciples, "Where shall we buy bread for these people to eat?" There were about five thousand men. Philip quickly calculated the costs of buying food for five thousand men just like I calculated my cost. My cost came out to $50,000. Philip's cost was eight months' wages of man. How much does a man make a month nowadays after tax? Suppose $4,000.

$4,000 x 8 = $32,000. Philip's answer was: We don't have that kind of money and so we can not feed the five thousand hungry men. I saw myself exactly like Philip. No, no, no, no. I should not be like Philip.

I should be like Andrew. Andrew brought Jesus five loaves of bread and two fish. The food belonged to a boy. How did Andrew persuade the boy to give up his food? It seemed like a key point to me. But the Bible did not explain how Andrew took the boy's food out of his hand. The Bible did not explain because it was not important. I interpreted it as receiving donations from others. And I did not want to do it. So I could not imitate Andrew either.

But I kept my prayers topics for sending books to prisons. I thought if I keep on praying to God, God may help me to make $50,000 and I can do it with my own money. You never know how the Lord will answer my prayers.

I attended CMI International Bible Conference 2024 in Dallas. I had an opportunity to speak about my book writing and publishing for fifteen minutes. I asked the audience to pray for me to send my books to all the prisons in Korea and in the U.S.A.

Gordon and Gail Smith who attended the conference, accepted this as their mission. After returning from the conference Gordon began to call prisons in Texas as many as he could. One prison chaplain responded. Gordon got a mailing address. The address started with Death Row. It was a prison that housed the prisoners who had death sentences.

Gordon, Gail and I studied Luke 23:30-43. Jesus was a death row prisoner. Two other death row prisoners were executed on the cross. One crucified criminal mocked Jesus. The other criminal believed that death is not the end but there will be life in Jesus' kingdom after his death.

This faith led him from eternal death to eternal life. On the cross he got a windfall jackpot.

He asked Jesus, "Jesus, remember me when you come into your kingdom." All the crimes he had ever committed were forgiven. Jesus accepted his faith. Jesus answered him, "I tell you the truth, today you will be with me in paradise." I pray that many death row prisoners may find the same jackpot and the same grace from Jesus. Their destination is not condemnation but paradise.

The Lord granted me Gordon and Gail Smith as my coworkers for prison ministry and we began to pray together over the phone. The Lord opened the door of sending my books to prisons.

Houston CMI church sent 25 books to the death row prison. I did not have $50,000. I thought that I could not send books to prisons. But the Lord granted Gordon and Gail to work together not with upfront money but with what we have, prayers and contacting prisons. With what we have, we have been approaching it step by step.

After prayers I decided to use my tithe money to send twenty books each month to prisons. Then I realized that it was five loaves of bread and two fish I am bringing to Jesus.

"How many loaves do you have?" he asked. "Go and see."

Mark 6:38

They brought five loaves of bread and two fish to Jesus. They could not figure out how these small amounts of food could feed five thousand men. Jesus accepted and blessed the five loaves of bread and two fish. The five loaves of bread and two fish kept on multiplying, multiplying, multiplying, probably inside of the distributing baskets, until all five thousand men ate and had left overs. Multiplying is not my part. My part was bringing my tithe to send books to prisons every month. This month I decided to send four books to four prisons. = 16 books.

But I could not order because my second book, 'The Half Basement' disappeared from Amazon.com. I had to wait until the book showed up again on Amazon.com. Gordon called Amazon. A woman answered that it was out of stock. But out of frustration I cried and Gail comforted me with her prayers.

I cried to the Lord, "Lord, I knew nothing about writing a book, nothing about publishing. You helped me until now. But this is too much for me. Please, come and solve this problem. I don't know what happened to the book. It is gone." Then the project manager said that there are some technical issues and it will be resolved in a week or so. I was relieved from stress and I stopped crying out to the Lord.

A couple of days ago I received a phone call from my friend, Mrs. Moon. She said that she wants to pay for the sixteen books that I was going to send to four prisons. My neighbor said that she has two Amazon gift cards and she wanted to use them to send my books to prisons.

I felt that the Lord Jesus had already begun to multiply the five loaves of bread and two fish which Gordon, Gail, and I brought to Jesus.

Chapter 15:
Jesus' Gospel vs My Gospel

When I had a series of illnesses my prayer became shorter and seldom, maybe 5-10 minutes a day. But when I was writing a book, my prayer was non stop and I had to ask the Lord constantly what to write and how to write. After writing two books I was filled with the spirit of prayer. My prayer life was strengthened to another level.

Morning prayer is mostly meditating on God; God the creator, God the Savior, God the Sovereign Lord. I meditate on God the Creator based on Genesis chapter one, God of Almighty power, God of love. With Almighty power and love God created the heavens and the earth in chaotic darkness. That's love.

Then I focus on the love of God. God's love is pure, holy, beautiful, almighty, resurrection, the fountain of all life, humble, greater than all our sins, commandment of love, and sacrificial. God gave His only Son as a sacrifice for our sins to die on the cross.

Then I meditate on Jesus on the cross. It's beyond my imagination that Jesus offered his life on the cross and suffered the punishment of sins that He did not commit. Jesus suffered the pain of death almost six hours on the cross and died saying His last words; it is finished. This part is beyond my comprehension. My human heart can not fathom the depth of the heart of Jesus. I only thank Jesus.

I confess to Jesus," Lord Jesus, You are my Savior." "Thank you for cleansing all my sins with your blood." After that confession I

91

move to Jesus' death, burial in a tomb, resurrection after three days, showing Himself for forty days to His disciples, ascension at the end of forty days, sitting at the right hand of God, praying and helping His people and His churches that are in this world, His coming back through the Rapture and the second coming to judge the world. My prayer finishes with, "Lord, remember me when You come back. I am here." I repeat these meditation and prayers every morning.

One day I was praying. "Thank you for cleansing all my sins with your blood." Then I should move to Jesus's death and burial in the tomb. But before I moved to Jesus' death. I saw the blood of Jesus moved from me, went to my enemies and cleansed all my enemies with His blood just as He did to me. It was something that I saw in my mind, not with my physical eyes.

I wondered and puzzled by what the Lord had just done. Something was not right. That was not what I believed.

I believed that Jesus washed all my sins with His blood and punished all my enemies. That's what I believed. They destroyed my marriage life and my family had to suffer. They should be punished. But instead of punishment Jesus washed them with His blood.

I heard not a single word from them asking forgiveness. Someone approached me with an apology and I refused. I refused to accept his approach of 'A MISTAKE AND APOLOGY.' I would accept if his attitude is A CONFESSION OF SIN AND ASKING FORGIVENESS.' There are huge differences between these two.

They should be punished by Jesus for their sins against me and my family. I was a victim. How could they be treated the same as me? Should a criminal and a victim be treated in the same way? That's not right.

But Jesus showed me that His blood washed not only me but also my enemies. I thought about this all day long. I came to a conclusion. I had a different gospel, my own gospel, different from the Gospel of Jesus.

My Own Gospel - Jesus Blood forgives all my sins, but Jesus punishes all my enemies.

Jesus Gospel - Jesus Blood forgives not only my sins but also the sins of my enemies.

I felt sorry because Jesus treated me and my enemies in the same way. But I found the reason. Jesus came into this world as the Savior of the world, as my Savior, as my enemies' Savior. Jesus is my Savior. Jesus is the Savior of my enemies, too.

There was Jesus' word I could neither understand nor obey. "Love your enemies and pray for those who persecute you." Matthew 5:44. In the perspective of Jesus as the Savior of the world I understood why Jesus said that. Jesus wants to save my enemies, too. By praying for my enemy I am joining with the work of Jesus who wants to save my enemy.

This God's teaching to me was ongoing lessons about forgiveness. It was like a step by step series, each step a little deeper into the meaning of forgiveness.

The conclusion and one point of my first book is forgiveness. I selected a passage from the Bible about forgiveness. I meditated on it, understood the meaning of it, and I wrote it confidently in the last chapter of the first book, 'I Asked The Author.'

This was my point: Because Jesus forgave us, we, too, should forgive our enemies. If we don't forgive, God will cancel His forgiveness of our sins. The books were printed, published, and went out into the world with this lesson. I wrote as if I knew everything about forgiveness. In the eyes of God I was just beginning. I just began to pay my attention truly to the meaning of forgiveness.

I knew in my head that I must forgive everyone who wronged against me. But in my heart I still had grudges. I was not aware that I had my own gospel different from the Gospel of Jesus. My own gospel was that Jesus Blood forgives all my sins but Jesus punishes my enemies. This my own gospel was blocking the flow of God's love of forgiveness. It was like a car stopped and blocked at a toll gate on an expressway. My own gospel was like a toll gate blocking the flow of God's forgiveness into my heart. My own gospel had to be removed. I was not aware of it, I could not do it, but Jesus did it by showing me His washing my enemies with His blood.

Since I accepted Jesus as the Savior of the world, not only my Savior but also the Savior of my enemies, I felt that my narrow mind became a little bigger and wider embracing more people. Welcoming people became natural and spontaneous. When I was a pastor, embracing others was a duty, an obligation, and a responsibility. I had to force myself to love others with my small heart. But when I had a bigger and wider heart, loving and embracing others became easy, natural, and joyful. My heart was changing.

Since then about 3-4 months passed, in the beginning of last June, after I understood and digested about my own gospel blocking Jesus' Gospel, the Lord taught me again about forgiveness, an even deeper meaning of forgiveness.

Some believers don't like dreams. So I try to minimize my stories about dreams. But when my dream is the only source to explain, I have no choice but to explain my dream. I will just copy what I wrote down.

The Deeper Meaning Of Forgiveness 06-06-2024 6:30am

In my dream I was inside of a bus. Inside of the bus there were young people, mostly young men of college age. The bus was not crowded, maybe half of the seats were occupied.

I was sitting in the front area of the bus because I was ready to get off. I had several plant pots with me. In the back of the bus somewhere the church leader was sitting. He looked young. He had a pure look that he had before corruption.

The bus was coming closer to my house. The bus was on the main street. In order to go to my house, the bus had to turn left. I did not want the bus to turn left to go to the street where my house was. I just wanted them to drop me off in the main street. Then I would move my plants pots one by one to my home. I had no problem taking care of my stuff.

But the bus turned to the left, arrived, and stopped in front of my house so that I did not have to carry my pots back and forth several times. This was done not by my request but by the consideration of the leader and his group in the bus. I did not expect that kind action from them. Their kindness made me feel uncomfortable. I did not want them to do it for me. Then I was woken up.

This dream made me think about the meaning of forgiveness.

The meaning of my forgiveness was; I forgave them.

I don't curse them anymore.

I don't curse their family anymore.

I don't hate them anymore.

But I had these strings attached to me; I don't want to be around them.

I don't want to see them.

I don't want to eat with them at the same table.

I don't want to be on the same bus with them.

Please, stay away from me and don't talk to me.

But in my dream they showed me their kindness and consideration by turning the bus and stopping in front of my house. No, no, no, no. Please, don't do that. Leave me alone. I am allergic to you all. Would you do me a favor? Leave me alone. I did not want to deal with them whatsoever. That was the meaning of forgiveness I thought and I had practiced.

What was the Lord trying to teach me through the dream? I forgave them but my mind was closed holding grudges. I did not want to have a friendship. And it was not forgiveness in the eyes of God. The Lord showed me what was lacking in me. I saw it through my dream. I would not be able to recognize my shortcomings unless I saw it in my dream. God wanted me to open my heart and start to have a friendship. That was a deeper meaning of forgiveness.

A friendship with them? No, no, no, no. I don't like it. I can not do it. I resisted the deeper meaning of forgiveness. I did not want to think about it. I closed my mind and ears. I avoided facing it. I ran far, far away from it because I did not want to deal with it.

Weeks later I came back to God's teaching and opened my mind a tiny bit about ⅛ inch. I accepted that the Lord is right. My narrow and small heart was not able to accept the Lord's teaching. But really, really, slowly I began to open my mind to people I kept distance from. I sat next to them, I initiated conversation and talked to them. So far I found they were really nice. I felt their warm hearts. I had joyful conversations with them. I tried and it was good.

The Lord is waiting for me to grow in the renewed friendship with people who wronged me in the past. I think that there is a lot more in God's forgiveness which my human mind can not comprehend now. Actually I am a little scared of the next deeper,

deeper meaning of forgiveness. The Lord did not jump but has been guiding me step by step gradually widening the capacity of my heart. Forgiveness is not something from knowing nothing to knowing the whole at once through study. It is a matter of heart. It is a process of growing from a human heart to God's heart, just like a baby grows to adulthood.

Later, I began to pray to the Lord for my readers of my books. After reading my books some readers may have a desire to come to the Lord. I prayed for them. I asked the Lord to accept them as His own, as His own son, as His own daughter, love them, and raise them as His own children.

Then I knew how hard it would be for the Lord to do it. I refused to restore a friendship with my enemies. I refused their offer of kindness. But I was asking the Lord to do what I refused to do.

It was like a father asked his daughter to do the right thing. She refused to do it. But then she asked her father to do the same thing she refused to do and even more. The Lord wanted me to have a friendship with an open heart and I ran away. I did not ask the Lord for friendship with sinners but adopt them as His own sons and daughters.

I had tears in my eyes as I asked the Lord to welcome and adopt sinners as His sons and daughters because I knew how hard it would be for God to do it. But I had to ask the Lord repeatedly to accept the readers who were coming to the Lord, not friendship but adoption.

We left our jobs, our family, and our country and went all over the world to preach the Gospel. What do we preach? We preach God's salvation, God's forgiveness through the blood of Jesus. How do we preach? We preach through teaching the words of God. We repeatedly teach the words of the Gospel again and again and again. Some day they will believe in God's forgiveness.

But what do we show them? Have we shown them what forgiveness is through our own life?

Or have we shown them our fight, bitterness, and breakup? Have we gone to other nations to show them our fight, breakup and unforgiveness? Or have we gone to the mission field to show them what forgiveness is through our own lives?

As for me, my answer is no, I haven't. I haven't shown them what forgiveness is. I didn't even know the meaning of it. I just began to learn the meaning of forgiveness.

Chapter 16:
What It Means To Live A Life

When I was a little girl in elementary school, I made a blueprint of my future life. I would make three million dollars first. At that time one million dollars had ten or hundreds times more value than today's million dollars.

I would use one million dollars for my family. I would buy land, and build a three story house. Let my parents, my brother and his family, my sisters and their families live in that house. I would use the second million to maintain the building and provide the necessities for my family. I would use the third million for my education and travel the world. I wanted to know and understand about the world I was living in. I wanted to study five languages and extensively travel the world not for sightseeing but for fundamental understanding about the world.

Gradually I began to realize it was not possible to make three million dollars. My reality was I did not make even three dollars. I had to let go of this dream.

Then I had a different approach to life. Suppose that I had an unlimited amount of money. Use the money for whatever I want to use it for. Because of the unlimited amount of money I did not have to wait for holiday sales and did not use discount coupons. It was all I was spending in my imagination. I bought a mansion, I bought cars, I bought clothes, and bags. I ate at the best restaurants. Then I did not know what to buy anymore. There was no more I wanted to buy.

Is that all? I expected more. But there was no more that money could do. So I began to observe super rich people to see how they spend their money. I found three things rich people always spend their money on; mansions, cars, a life of debauchery.

In my imagination I was a billionaire. I spent as much money as I wanted. I did not find paradise, instead I found disappointment and an empty end. A lot of money requires constant maintenance, safe keeping and fear. My thirst for making a lot of money was quenched. I was content with a house to live in, one car and three meals a day. I had something else to do with my life.

Yet almost everyone on earth tries to be rich. All activities and struggles of people are aiming at money, money, and money. To make more money people compromise and servile, lie and deceive, flirt and seduce, kill and be killed. How many people amassed as much money as they wanted to have? Did they find that money brought them happiness?

Life is once. It is not something to experiment with or just follow what others do.

Then I turned to the truth, the world of God and eternity. First, I had to find God. My thirsty search for God lasted six years without success and God came to me in seventh year. It was a shift from the visual physical world to the invisible spiritual world.

It was unlimited. The invisible spiritual world is unlimited, endlessly open, into the world of God. It was not like the disappointing end of money. I put my life into it. My struggle was to live my life according to the words of the Bible.

God's will goes ahead of creation of a creature.

"Let there be light" and there was light.

In Genesis chapter one all things were created in this order.

God commanded a specific creature to exit and the creature came to exit..

I am not different. Let there be Boksoon Kim and I came to exist.

Life is to find God's purpose that preceded my existence and fulfill it.

I am the only one who can fulfill the purpose of my existence.

Through all environments I grew up in, I have been molded and prepared to fulfill my purpose.

The purpose of God in my life was to preach God's salvation in Toledo and in Houston.

Then my life crumbled down by the united power of jealousy and I had to deal with forgiveness.

While writing about forgiveness in chapter fifteen of this book, I realized how my narrow unforgiving mind was changing wider and bigger as I understood the deeper meaning of forgiveness. Hatred was leaving slowly. Love and compassion were filling in. My human heart was gradually sliding into the heart of God.

Then I realized the meaning of life.

What it means to live a life is changing from the human heart into God's heart.

The quantity of life, visual tangible possessions are temporary. The ownership moves from hand to hand, from person to person, from nation to nation. Death terminates ownership of all possessions.

But the quality of heart remains with me forever. The quality of my heart is truly mine. It will be my eternal possession and my eternal image.

There are expressions about different men's hearts.

He is a saint.

He is an angel.

He is kind.

He is an animal.

He is worse than an animal.

These expressions show to what degree the person has a human heart in him and to what degree God's heart in him. The difference comes from knowing the meaning of God's forgiveness and practicing it. That's what it means to live a life.

Life is not accumulating and gathering possessions. Life is to clean up the animal human heart and to grow in the pure heart of God. It is what it means to live a life. I am the only one who can do it for myself. We have time to do it during our lifetime. Yet one may die as a saint, and one may die as one worse than an animal.

"Multitudes who sleep in the dust of the earth will awake; some to everlasting life, others to shame and everlasting contempt. Those who are wise will shine like the brightness of the heavens, and those who lead many to righteousness, like the stars for ever and ever."

Daniel 12:2,3

I want to shine like the brightness of the heavens in eternity. I found the way to do it.

Made in the USA
Columbia, SC
27 November 2024

47730603R00059